ADVERTISING IN THE NEWS

ADRIAN HADLAND, LESLEY COWLING & BATE FELIX TABI TABE

PAID-FOR CONTENT AND THE SOUTH AFRICAN PRINT MEDIA

HSRC PRESS

Compiled by the Society, Culture and Identity Research Programme of the Human Sciences Research Council in association with the Media Observatory, research arm of Wits Journalism

Published by HSRC Press
Private Bag X9182, Cape Town, 8000, South Africa
www.hsrcpress.ac.za

First published 2007

ISBN 978-07969-2183-3

© 2007 Human Sciences Research Council

Copy edited by David Merrington
Typeset by Robin Taylor
Cover design by Jenny Frost
Print management by comPress

Distributed in Africa by Blue Weaver
Tel: +27 (0) 21 701 4477; Fax: +27 (0) 21 701 7302
www.oneworldbooks.com

Distributed in Europe and the United Kingdom by Eurospan Distribution Services (EDS)
3 Henrietta Street, Covent Garden, London, WC2E 8LU, United Kingdom
Tel: +44 (0) 20 7240 0856; Fax: +44 (0) 20 7379 0609
www.eurospangroup.com/bookstore

Distributed in North America by Independent Publishers Group (IPG)
Call toll-free: (800) 888 4741; Fax: +1 (312) 337 5985
www.ipgbook.com

CONTENTS

List of tables and figures   iv
Acknowledgements   v
Abbreviations and acronyms   vi

1   Introduction   1

2   Literature review   5

3   The South African context   13

4   Methodology   17

5   Case studies   19

6   Focus groups   47

7   Interviews with magazine managers   51

8   Regulation   57

9   Conclusion   63

References   67

LIST OF TABLES AND FIGURES

Table

Table 5.1   Breakdown of advertisement features carried in *The Star*, March 2005   42

Figures

Figure 5.1   *Audio Video*: Publishing, editorial, advertising and management structure   28

Figure 5.2   *Audio Video*: Income streams as a percentage of total income   29

Figure 5.3   *Audio Video*: Advertising/editorial spillover   32

Figure 5.4   *Audio Video*: Percentage of linked news content   33

Figure 5.5   *Audio Video*: Percentage of linked review content   34

ACKNOWLEDGEMENTS

The authors would like to acknowledge the work and efforts of Wits students Nicola Mawson and Ndaba Dlamini, who conducted and wrote up two of the case studies. The funding for this project came primarily from the HSRC's parliamentary grant with assistance from the National Research Foundation. The authors would like to thank the media companies, editors and managers who cooperated with this project, including Moegsien Williams, editor of *The Star* newspaper, Lorain Tulleken of the Independent Newspaper group's Special Projects department, Terry Meyer, Andrew Cuthbertson, Dean Schoeman, Bob Pryers and the team at *Audio Video*, and Colleen Naude and Tian Liebenberg of *Finweek*.

We interviewed Mike Tissong, general manager of Johnnic Communications Media Magazine Division, Debbie McIntyre, advertising manager of Caxton Magazines, Jane Raphaely, the doyenne of South African magazine publishing, CEO of Associate Magazines and publisher of the South African *Cosmopolitan*, as well as Andrew Sneddon, Elsa Carpenter-Frank and Andrew Gillet of Touchline Publishing, a division of Media24 Magazines. Thanks also to Professor Anton Harber, and reviewers Dr Herman Wasserman and Robert Brand, for comments on the draft version.

ABBREVIATIONS AND ACRONYMS

ASASA	Advertising Standards Authority of South Africa
LSM	Living Standards Measure
POSA	Press Ombudsman of South Africa
Sanef	South African National Editors' Forum
SAARF	South African Advertising Research Foundation

CHAPTER 1

Introduction

> Credibility is good business.
> (*Meyer 2004: 82*)

South African newspapers and magazines found themselves operating under increasingly difficult conditions in the 1990s, with an explosion of new media products and the entry of global media companies into the local market (Taylor 2002; Ensor 2001).[1] Although many media companies have posted enormous profits in the last few years, publications face stiff competition, not just for readers, but for advertising, which provides commercial media with the greater part of their revenue (Van Ginneken 1998). To maintain their profitability, many publications have developed a range of strategies to attract advertising. In particular, these strategies include developing the kind of content that advertisers most desire – content that creates a 'buying mood' for their products (Herman & Chomsky 1994: 17). These include niched supplements, special sections and advertorial pages (also known as surveys). Along with increasing their 'paid-for content', however, many publications appear to be failing to signal adequately to readers when the content they are reading has been paid for by advertisers and when it has not. In addition, certain kinds of content carried in publications purely to attract advertising cannot easily be identified as such.

It is the authors' contention that the blurring of editorial content and advertising copy has a number of profoundly negative consequences. These range from the gradual erosion of public trust in the media and the 'poisoning' of public discourse (O'Neill 2002, lecture 5: 3) to the creation of impediments to the consolidation of our new democracy. Apart from these potential societal ills, we also argue that the growing practice of linking content to advertising in ways that are obscured from the reader can, if left unchecked, have commercial implications, damaging the credibility of titles and therefore affecting their profitability and long-term financial health.

As in most democracies, the print media in South Africa are self-regulating. The Press Code of Professional Practice (referred to from here on as the press code), policed by the Press Ombudsman of South Africa (POSA), is the principal mechanism for the self-regulation of the print media sector. The press code demands truth, accuracy and fairness from the media, together with a lack of distortion and misrepresentation.[2] The press code makes no mention of the treatment of advertising in newspapers or magazines. Regulation in this respect is instead to be found in the Advertising Standards Authority of South Africa's (ASASA) code, to which all South African newspapers and magazines are signatories. Several sections of the ASASA code deal with the labelling or identification of paid-for content, and specific requirements are spelt out to ensure that readers are not mislead. However, these aspects of the ASASA code are generally not enforced in the South African print media. Formal complaints

---

1 See chapter 3 for a fuller discussion of the commercial challenges facing newspapers and magazines.
2 For the full press code, see the website of the press ombudsman at www.ombudsman.org.za/content/default.asp.

to ASASA about the blurring of advertising and editorial in the print media are extremely rare. If formal complaints are not received, ASASA is powerless to act.

The freedom of media to report on a range of issues is enshrined in the country's legal system on the basis of a constitutional provision for freedom of expression, which the media are seen to safeguard (Louw 2005: 121–130). The legal provisions that concern the media stress the importance of truth and accuracy, as do the ethical codes of practice in newsrooms. However, few of these codes make a direct comment on the treatment of advertising material in newspapers and magazines. If, as the press code suggests, 'vigilant self-regulation' truly is 'the hallmark of a free and independent press', very serious questions need to be asked about the extent to which commercial media regulate and manage paid-for content, and whether the industry needs to consider creating, adapting or enforcing existing codes to set general guidelines for ethical behaviour in this regard. To address these questions, it is important to consider what is happening in practice in publications across the country.

It has long been journalistic practice, particularly in newspapers, to divide content into two distinctly recognisable categories: editorial, which is written for readers, and advertising, which is paid for by advertisers who seek to draw the attention of those readers to their goods. Advertising is usually packaged in display ads of various sizes, but, where advertising content is presented in the style of reports or articles – known as advertorial in the trade and often written by journalists – the convention has been to signal the status of such reports to the reader. Many publications still indicate such content, displaying labels such as 'Special', 'Survey', 'Advertorial' or 'Commercial feature' at the beginning of the section. Such signalling is supposedly a means of letting readers know that this content is not produced according to the norms and standards of the editorial sections and has been paid for by an advertiser, which allows readers to judge it accordingly. However, some of this signalling actually obscures the nature of the copy, such as labelling a section 'Special feature'. It is not at all clear that readers generally understand what this labelling means and whether they can identify what advertorial copy is even when it is signalled. Therefore, when considering this practice, it is important to take into account what readers make of such content.

The division of content into editorial and advertising has been paralleled in the day-to-day running of publications (particularly newspapers), in which there has been a separation between advertising sales and editorial departments. In magazines, the line has traditionally been less rigid, with advertising and editorial departments having more to do with each other. The balancing act of dividing editorial and advertising functions is seen as a particularly important protection for the integrity of a news publication, and journalists have often fiercely resisted any assaults on their autonomy over editorial decisions. Recently, concerns have been raised in South African media circles about whether this division (commonly known as the 'Chinese Wall') is under threat. However, some media executives have argued that the strict separation of the advertising and editorial functions is no longer appropriate in the new business climate, and have advocated more integration of editorial and marketing (see Harber 2004).

Contemporary research on the role of the media suggests that the aggressive pursuit of commercial gains by credible publications (rather than publications that rely on sensationalism and celebrity gossip) could be a short-term and dangerous state of affairs. As Philip Meyer points out in his important work, *The Vanishing Newspaper*, if readers no longer trust a newspaper or magazine, they will look elsewhere for the information they need (Meyer 2004). Over the medium to long term, this will diminish circulation, ultimately leading to a drop in advertising revenue. Advertisers of certain products also value the credibility of the media in which they place advertising, as they believe the environment in which the ads are placed can affect the way in which they are received by readers.

While the hard commercial reality indicates that a loss of trust could translate directly into print media companies' bottom lines, it is also true on a more philosophical level that misrepresentation, deceit and the general whittling away of trust do nothing to support new institutions, tolerance, understanding, debate in the public domain, or the strength of democratic rights and responsibilities. As eminent political philosopher Onora O'Neill argues, nothing damages trust like deception:

> If we deceive we make others our victims, and undermine or distort their possibilities for acting and communicating. We arrogantly base our own communication and action on principles that destroy trust, and so limit others' possibilities for action. Ways of communicating can be unacceptable for many reasons; threats may intimidate and coerce; slander may injure. But the most common wrong done in communicating is deception, which undermines and damages others' capacities to judge and communicate, to act and to place trust with good judgement. Duties to reject deception are duties for everyone: for individuals and for government and for institutions and professions – including the media and journalists. (O'Neill 2002, lecture 5: 5)

It is the authors' contention that, while not always deliberate or even conscious, the blurring of advertising and editorial is an act of deceit and misrepresentation that undermines the integrity of the media. As O'Neill says, 'the press has no license to deceive; and we have no reasons to think that a free press needs such a licence' (O'Neill 2002, lecture 5: 5). The print media sector in South Africa, in the battle to survive over the last ten years, appears to have pushed the boundaries at every opportunity, particularly in the area of paid-for content. This research intends to test this perception through a number of small and connected projects that investigate key aspects of the issues we have raised.

First, we set out to examine whether certain South African publications are increasingly selling packages to advertisers that link editorial content and advertising in ways that obscure the origin of the content, and what kind of strategies they make use of. We looked at three publications – a mainstream newspaper, a finance magazine and a highly niched electronic magazine – in order to establish how much editorial content is linked to advertisers, how this is made evident to the reader (if at all) and whether this is a growing trend in these publications. We also attempted to map the variety of strategies used by different publications to attract and retain advertising.

Although these findings are not generalisable to all publications, the focus on particular cases allowed us to look closely at the micro-level of day-to-day business practices, and also to examine actual content. The interviews with decision makers at these publications also allowed us to record their perceptions of whether such strategies are becoming widespread in the industry as they monitor the actions of their competitors. For a broader perspective, we surveyed magazine and newspaper publishing companies to determine, in general, what kinds of strategy they use across their publications to attract and manage advertising, and also to establish whether these media organisations have codes of conduct or guidelines concerning the publication of linked content.

Second, the research included focus groups, to observe how readers read a publication and, specifically, how they relate to paid-for content and special sections. An important aspect of the focus-group research was to find out whether readers are generally able to recognise paid-for content or paid-for sections when they are labelled, and what their attitude is to such sections.

Finally, we looked at the codes and guidelines used by the industry to regulate journalistic practice in order to establish whether there are any principles that may have a bearing on the responsibilities the print media have to their readers with regard to advertising content.

The aim of this research project, initiated by the Human Sciences Research Council's Society, Culture and Identity research programme and supported by the University of the Witwatersrand's Media Observatory, was to identify and understand trends that may diminish media quality, and to enhance debate within the industry about ways in which to manage growing commercial pressures. Funding came from a parliamentary grant to the HSRC and from the National Research Foundation. We hope the results of the expenditure of public money will encourage media companies, managers and advertisers (including government) to examine the practices that currently exist in attracting advertising and consider the implications for credibility and for readers. As long as the media constitute a self-regulating entity, change can only come from within.

CHAPTER 2

Literature review

> The challenge is not to stay in business; it is to stay in journalism.
> (*Harold Evans, former editor of the* London Sunday Times) [3]

The complex relationship between the media's commercial and public interest functions has been the subject of much academic inquiry over the years. On one hand, producing news is a commercial enterprise, operating in accordance with the demands of the marketplace and the necessities of economic survival. On the other hand, newspapers and broadcasters also perceive themselves as vital to the functioning of society, responsible for informing citizens about all the significant issues and events they need to know about in order to make choices in a democracy (Schudson 1995; McManus 1994).

The liberal pluralist notion that the commercial and public service aspects of the media can be balanced, and that the commercial media guarantee a freedom from the state (Siebert, Peterson & Schramm 1956; McQuail 1987), has been challenged from a number of quarters over the last 150 years. Early Marxist critics saw the commercial media as part of a broader societal system that promoted the interests and ideologies of the dominant class in society. In the 1930s, the theorists of the Frankfurt School expressed concern about what they saw as the enormous impact of the growing mass media on society – media they saw as entertainment-driven and culturally bankrupt. These notions were developed further in the work of Dallas Smythe in his seminal 1981 work, *Dependency Road*. Smythe argued that the mass media were the 'systemic invention' of monopoly capitalism and had been devised to mass-produce audiences:

> The capitalist system cultivates the illusion that the three streams of information and things are independent: the advertising merely 'supports' or 'makes possible' the news, information, and entertainment, which in turn are separate from the consumer goods and services we buy. This is untrue. The commercial mass media are advertising in their entirety. (Smythe 1981: 7–8)

More recently, there has been a sustained critique of the commercial and globalised media from critical political economy theorists, who argue that the media's responsibilities to their readers and to society have been eroded by the way big media companies do business. A critical political economy of the media takes the position that 'different ways of financing and organising cultural production have traceable consequences for the range of discourses and representations in the public domain and for audiences' access to them' (Golding & Murdock 2000). Any examination of the media's role in society, therefore, would need to examine their dependence on advertising for revenue.

An important work on this topic was *Power without Responsibility* (Curran & Seaton 1991). Here the authors demonstrated the immense power of advertisers to limit 'the

---

[3] Quoted in Bagdikian 2000: 137.

variety of expression', and to 'conscript ... the press to the social order' (1991: 1, 9). Curran and Seaton argued that 'Advertisers acquire a de facto licensing authority since, without their support, newspapers ceased to be economically viable' (see Herman & Chomsky 1994: 14). Edward Herman and Noam Chomsky's influential work *Manufacturing Consent* also drew some powerful conclusions about the interconnectedness of the media, major corporations, the financial sector and government. The current state of affairs, they argued, was witness to the development of an 'advertising-based' media system that skewed the news agenda, safeguarded corporate interests and propagated commercial values. Herman and Chomsky posited that such a system 'will gradually increase advertising time and marginalise or eliminate altogether programming that has significant public affairs content' (Herman & Chomsky 1994: 22).

One of the most outspoken critics of the relationship between advertising and the media has been Ben Bagdikian, former prize-winning journalist and now academic. According to Bagdikian:

> [a]dvertising is not a luxury to large corporations but an activity with profound economic and political consequences. The media are now dependent upon these corporations for most of their revenues and increasingly they are owned by such corporations. The media have become partners in achieving the social and economic goals of their patrons and owners. Yet it is the newspapers, general magazines and broadcasters who are citizens' primary source of information and analysis of precisely this kind of economic and political issue. This raises the question of whether our mass media are free to exercise their traditional role of mediating among the forces of society at a time when they have become an integral part of one of these forces. (Bagdikian 2000: 151)

Historically, there has been a wall of separation between the newsroom and the commercial operations of media companies, the product of what Bagdikian refers to as 'centuries of tension between the purity of news and the greed of publishers' (Bagdikian 2000 xxvi). However, he argues that economic developments in the last 50 years have made advertisers more powerful in negotiating terms for their business. Indeed, some now argue that the so-called 'wall of separation' has become so porous it barely exists at all (Leonard, 2000).

The economic developments to which Bagdikian refers include the concentration of the media worldwide into increasingly few large corporations. Political economist, Vincent Mosco, observes that concentration has heralded the 'growing integration of the news and entertainment industries, blurring the distinction between informational and commercial content' (Mosco 1996: 90). Concentration has also diminished competition, 'the deus ex machina of liberal theory which makes the consumer sovereign and proprietors accountable' (Curran & Seaton 1991: 282).

Another trend that has influenced the media has been the rise of niching, which has seen a move from creating products for mass audiences to targeting 'an identifiable group with predictable habits' (Schudson 1984: 63–66). In most countries, adspend is largely directed towards groups that are more affluent (1984: 28). In South Africa, advertisers tend to rely heavily on the Living Standards Measure (LSM) – a demographic tool developed more than 15 years ago by the South African Advertising Research Foundation (SAARF) to measure the standard of living of audiences – and more than 65 per cent of adspend is directed at less than 36 per cent of the population (Cowling 2004). However, audiences can also be targeted by linking advertising of particular products or services to editorial content that covers such products, or to the context in which such products and services are offered, such as travel, health and beauty, and personal finance sections.

Advertisers also prefer content that creates 'a buying mood' (Herman & Chomsky 1994: 17), so niching can lead to a situation where content must be generally positive. Women's magazines, for example, must run stories on make-up and beauty products to attract the advertisers of those products. The experience of *MS* magazine, which tried to attract such advertisers on the basis of the audience they could deliver without running the associated content, showed the futility of trying to buck the system (Steinem 1990). Closer to home, Ann Donald, the editor of *Fair Lady*, was prevented from running a story on beauty products that were ineffective, ostensibly because the magazine had advertisers whose products were mentioned in the exposé.[4]

In the 1960s, American commentator Richard Maisel observed that the mass media system appeared to be fragmenting, or becoming more specialised, relative to the rest of the economy (cited in Meyer 2004: 2). This trend has been clearly discernible in the South African media environment. In the commercial magazine sector, for instance, the number of titles has almost doubled in the last decade, and the number of radio stations has grown enormously (SAARF 2006). Fragmentation and competition, some argue, makes media deeply vulnerable to the dictates of commercialism. According to Louw (2001), 'Most niches are still run according to the logic of top-down, manipulative communication, produced by professional communicators who target that niche to generate profits for their employers. Increasingly these employers are global media corporations' (Louw 2001: 99). Bagdikian, too, observes that 'magazines are increasingly special-interest ones, often created solely to carry advertisements to a target audience' (Bagdikian 2000: 132).

There have certainly been commentators who have argued the case that there is nothing wrong with the print media using their products to generate as much profit as possible (Crotty 2006). Each print organisation is a business, after all, seeking to generate value and growth for shareholders and sustainability and income for employees. What's wrong with that?

The difficulty is that newspapers and magazines are not packaging materials that have a neutral or absent political, economic or even constitutional role. The print

---

4 Cream of the crap, *Noseweek* 75, January 2006.

media form part of the balance of powers; they contribute to the definition of what Jurgen Habermas (1989) called the public sphere and are an important point of contact between the state and the people. Hester Lockyear, in a recent article in the journal *Communicatio*, argues that 'The domination of the public sphere [an open space where rational political discourse between economy and state can take place] by commercialism has a direct influence on the construction of meaning' (Lockyear 2004: 29). 'People look to the media for guidance in discovering public meanings and definitions. Social and cultural identity lies at the heart of the construction of meaning by the media' (2004: 29). McQuail, too, argues that 'the higher dependence on advertising as a source of revenue, the less independent the content of the cultural production' (cited in Lockyear 2004: 29).

Magazines may seem to be exempted, by virtue of their lifestyle nature, from providing information necessary to citizenship or from constituting a space where matters of national importance are debated. However, they still need to take into account the expectations of their readers. Magazine readers may not necessarily want to be informed about issues defined as in the public interest, but they may rely on the publication for advice and information of a more personal or specialist nature, and would expect that publication to be truthful and accurate.

Few more powerful arguments on the subject of truth in public life can be found than in the Reith lectures delivered in 2002 by prominent political philosopher Onora O'Neill. 'We need to pay more attention to the accuracy of information provided to the public,' O'Neill said by way of introducing the first of her five lectures (O'Neill 2002 lecture 1: 2). She went on to argue that deception and misinformation could not only mislead the public but undermine the trust and truth that are the foundations of society.

> If powerful institutions are allowed to publish, circulate and promote material without indicating what is known and what is rumour; what is derived from a reputable source and what is invented, what is standard analysis and what is speculation; which sources may be knowledgeable and which are probably not, they damage our public culture and all our lives. (O'Neill 2002 lecture 5: 4)

O'Neill goes on to suggest,

> ... if we can't trust what the press report, how can we tell whether to trust those on whom they report? An erratically reliable or unassessable press might not matter for privileged people with other sources of information. They can tell which stories are near the mark and which are confused, vicious or simply false; but for most citizens it matters. How can we tell whether newspapers, web sites and publications that claim to be 'independent' are not, in fact, promoting some agenda? How can we tell whether and when we are on the receiving end of hype and spin, of misinformation and disinformation? ... If the media mislead, or if readers cannot assess their reporting, the wells of public discourse and public life are poisoned. (O'Neill 2002: 3)

There is evidence, too, that declining levels of trust or confidence in the media rebound onto the body politic. In a major study conducted in the 1980s by William Schneider and Martin Lipset, the authors demonstrated that, when the public has confidence in the press, it also has confidence in the government (cited in Meyer, 2004: 71).

Many other authors have grappled with the notion of trust and its importance in the interface between reader and title, as well as between citizen and state. Curran and Seaton (1991) suggest that the media have 'an authoritative relationship with their audience' based on 'dependence and trust'. This relationship then provides the media with a potentially independent power base in society, a base that has been growing more powerful in recent years (Curran & Seaton 1991: 262). Several authors, including Garnham (1990), Becker (1989) and Mansell (1993), have interrogated the threat to public life (sometimes called the 'democracy gap') in which the re-organisation of telecommunications along market lines and to suit consumers has not addressed the needs of citizens (cited in Mosco 1996: 113).

Trust is, however, not merely an element that, once lost, weakens the public sphere or compromises citizenship. Philip Meyer argues in *The Vanishing Newspaper* that trust is a key element in the profitability and sustainability of newspaper companies and their titles. 'There is no shortage of historical studies showing a correlation between quality journalism and business success' (Meyer 2004: 1). In a review of 35 years of academic literature on the topic, conducted on behalf of the American Society of Newspaper Editors (ASNE) in 2003, Esther Thorson concluded that 'the preponderance of large-scale US studies support[s] the connection between newspaper content, circulation and penetration and overall financial health' (Thorson, 2003a: 3).

The literature is indeed rich and varied on the subject. Landmark studies include Leo Bogart's 1977 survey of 746 editors and his isolation of 23 indicators of newspaper quality (Bogart 1989), work by Stone, Stone and Trotter (1981) showing a correlation between editorial quality and circulation, Picard's investigation of the impact of economic pressures on newspaper quality (Picard 1985), Gladney's study of newspaper excellence (Gladney 1990), and the follow-up work on Bogart by Lacy and Fico (1991) and Kim (2005). All of these, together with the body of work they represent and associated studies, indicate that, in Thorson's words, 'investment in quality content improves the bottom line' (Thorson 2003a: 3). Thorson told the ASNE convention in 2003 that one study in the mid 1980s used eight different measures of quality from 114 daily newspapers. The study concluded that 'about 22 per cent of the variation in circulation was related to the measures of quality' (Thorson 2003b: 2).

While there is broad consensus on this hypothesis, it is worth noting that there remains considerable debate over a precise definition of editorial quality, as well as on the import of the range of complicating factors that blur the causality. Meyer argues that the causality is, in any case, less important than the accumulative result:

> Correlation doesn't prove causation, nor does it tell its direction. Maybe quality leads to success, or maybe success pays for quality. I'm arguing that it goes both ways. It's a reinforcing loop. When things go well, it's a virtuous circle. When they go badly, it's a vicious cycle. (Meyer 2003: 5)

In addition, while few of the studies made the distinction, quality content does not necessarily exclude tabloid newspapers, for whom the objectives of good writing, ease of access and a high proportion of local coverage (among the top Bogart indicators) most certainly apply.

> Quality can be thought about either in terms of how resources are allocated or by content. Both measures have different kinds of benchmarks. Resource allocation can be indexed by measures like size of the newshole,[5] number of editorial staff and number of wire services. Content can be indexed by accuracy, amount of local news and markers of depth of coverage, like backgrounders, investigative stories and issues-focused reporting. (Thorson 2003b)

In Bogart's important study, and supported by more recent research that has sought to contemporise his work, it is worth noting that integrity and editorial independence (as well as the ratio of editorial to advertising material in newspapers) were cited by newspaper editors surveyed as among the half dozen most important indicators of quality and therefore considered critical to long-term financial success (Bogart 1989, Lacy & Fico 1991, Sooyoung Choo 2004). Meyer, too, argues that the relationship of trust that is established by a newspaper's integrity and independence is vital both to its function as a public asset and to its profitability:

> The way to achieve societal influence is to obtain public trust by becoming a reliable and high-quality information provider ... the resulting higher quality earns more public trust in the newspaper, and not only larger readership and circulation but also influence with which advertisers will want their names associated. (Meyer 2004: 20)

Meyer has been able to demonstrate in quantitative terms how improving trust has been able to promote business success and growth. In a huge study of newspapers in 26 American counties, he demonstrates how a one-point improvement in trust (which he defines as credibility) is worth a 2.5 per cent increase in a newspaper's asking price for advertising. In addition, trust is also a key factor in building a strong market position: 'Trust, in a busy marketplace, lends itself to monopoly' (Meyer 2004: 43).

The importance of focusing on trust-raising strategies, as called for by Meyer, has been acknowledged in the local marketplace. According to *Sunday Times* publisher, Mike Robertson:

---

5 Rick Edmonds defines the 'newshole' as the balance between advertising and editorial copy, usually measured in column inches (Edmonds 2004: 5).

> In 1990, 30% of our readers said they trusted the *Sunday Times*. It was 50% by 1996 and by 2002 was up to 92% ... We did it by imposing stringent accuracy tests on our copy. We drummed it in ... We decided that even if meant that stories weren't quite as sexy and were toned down, our most important mission was to get things right.[6]

Meyer would also argue that, in addition to trustworthiness being a key factor in profitability, 'truth-telling is the basic value of journalism'.

The literature is in fact full of warnings of the potential dangers of mixing advertising and editorial. 'Threats to media freedom can come from within as easily as from without,' suggests Frank Morgan in an article entitled 'The price of freedom' (Morgan 2004: 16). According to Morgan, the media constitute one of those spaces in which society can and should sort out its concerns and priorities free from the power of the state and big business. 'But puzzles arise: one when the media themselves become big business; another when the media rely on the power of the state to ensure their freedom' (2004: 16). Morgan suggests that the way to protect the media's capacity to act as agents of communication between citizens is for journalists to be aware of 'what is legal, what is moral, and what is ethical in what they do' (2004: 23).

Even Rupert Murdoch, the press baron whom many accuse of undermining the traditional tenets of quality journalism, conceded in 2002 that 'good content is good business' (cited in Morgan 2004: 20). It is a conclusion that has built up not only anecdotal support among editors and publishers but demonstrable proof as provided by a number of quantitative studies conducted by the international academic community. Meyer can be no more explicit than this: 'Cutbacks in quality will erode public trust, weaken societal influence and eventually devastate circulation and advertising' (Meyer 2004: 20).

---

6 This information was taken from an interview with Mike Robertson by the writer, Adrian Hadland, in 2005, conducted as part of original research in pursuit of a PhD. Quotes used here by permission.

CHAPTER 3

The South African context

South Africa's transformation into a democratic state in 1994 seemed to herald a new era for media, one in which the media could finally fulfil a public interest role, providing information to all citizens and operating to protect the public. But, in spite of obvious shifts in media ownership, some moves toward diversification and the deregulation of the broadcasting sector, it wasn't long before commentators were beginning to question the depth and significance of change in the media sector. Sean Jacobs argued that the legacy of colonialism and apartheid on mass media development in South Africa continued to impact on the nature of the public sphere long after the formal end of apartheid. In fact, he observed that changes to the media environment in the post-1994 period had not been that far-reaching, nor had they led to the expected improvement in representation or democratic participation (Jacobs 2004: 17).

While the extent and significance of change in the media industry remains contested (see Tomaselli and Burger, cited in Harber 2002), there has been growing concern expressed within government and ruling political party circles that the South African mainstream media have become increasingly dependent on the forces of globalisation and commercialism. This has created a media industry that is not interested, or capable, of giving a voice to the voiceless or in representing the views or aspirations of the increasingly large proportion of South African society that is poor. President Thabo Mbeki, head of government communications Joel Netshitenzhe, Arts and Culture Minister Pallo Jordan and the former chairman of the portfolio committee on communication, Nat Kekana, have all spoken out on this perceived trend and its likely consequences.

At a South African National Editors' Forum (Sanef) meeting two years ago, Netshitenzhe described the need for media to make money as 'a real threat to media freedom'. The threat, he said, came from 'the bottom line', the demand for profit above all else by media owners. This 'ubiquitous' new 'deity' was making advertisers and marketers 'the kings of content', increasingly influencing editorial content (Harber 2004).

This was a warning that Mbeki also voiced in an address to the All Africa Editors' Conference in 2003. Mbeki similarly linked the increasing concentration of the media to threats to the integrity of the media: 'This threat, I would contend, is as dangerous – if not more so – than that posed by government' (Duncan 2003: 3). Mbeki's critique of the media, Duncan argues, reflects a debate about the deficiencies of the media that has been taking place for some time within government and African National Congress circles. It is an attitude that underpins high-level government wishes for a more 'responsive' media industry that is less hostile to the ANC and to government (Harber 2002). It also illustrates the political and social backdrop to this study.

In 2001, Kekana told parliament that the advertising business was largely unregulated, yet commanded huge budgets, which determined 'what and who create, develop, package and distribute content of television, radio and print' (Koenderman 2001). The argument has also been made that this dependence on advertising has caused a dumbing down of content and, as argued by other government figureheads, the marginalisation of large numbers of people not considered desirable by advertisers. One current newspaper editor, Mathatha Tsedu of *City Press*, has described this as 'red-lining readers', likening the process to the banks' practice in the 1990s of refusing to lend money to the poor (Duncan 2003). The debate has come to represent a divide within the South African media itself. One group treats government incursions into the media with extreme suspicion, as an attempt to reign in the watchdog role of the media, reduce their independence, and delegitimise them in order to pave the way for statutory regulation; the other group appears to be investing the national interest with new respectability and seeking to build a united, inclusive nation around common values (Duncan 2003). The debate is also illustrative of a campaign by social movements internationally to put non-commercial media on the agenda and to create free-speech radio and television stations as spaces for non-commercial journalism (Duncan 2003).

Kekana instituted hearings into the South African advertising industry to investigate the concern that advertisers were placing advertisements only in some publications and not in others. Media executives argued that the decisions of media buyers were biased against black media, and there was initially some talk of regulation of the advertising industry. However, advertisers argued that most of the products they were trying to sell were luxury goods, which meant that much of their business was focused on the affluent, and that this was the reason why media products that served the poor – still largely black in this country – were being marginalised. The question of advertorial and paid-for content was not canvassed, and the question of regulation was dropped. However, the hearings demonstrated that the commercial media's dependence on advertising is enormous, that it can affect the profitability and even the survival of newspapers that have big audiences and that poor audiences are marginalised as a result. It also demonstrates that Bagdikian's point about the increasing power of advertisers in the United States to dictate the terms for placing their business could be appropriate to local conditions (Bagdikian 2000).

Changes in South African society have had a significant impact on the relationship between editorial and advertising interests. The entry of the country in the 1990s into a global economy saw the arrival of international media companies, ready to compete with local publications for readers and advertisers, and the introduction of local versions of international magazine franchises, such as *Elle*, *Cosmopolitan* and *GQ*. There was also enormous growth in local media, particularly in broadcasting, which gave advertisers a much wider choice of vehicle for their advertisements, and which has fragmented audiences. In the late 1990s and the early 2000s, media managers began developing strategies to deal with reduced adspend, which included looking 'beyond traditional advertising revenue' (Taylor 2002).

In addition, advertisers and marketers trying to reach potential consumers changed the way they did business, in line with an international trend to target potential buyers through niched products. Advertisers also like to place their ads in an environment that is more likely to create a 'buying mood'. In the face of such challenges, many media companies have developed particular strategies to make their products more appealing to advertisers. One such strategy is to link editorial content to advertising and sell that as a package to advertisers, thereby satisfying the advertisers' need to target. This may take the form of introducing sections into the publication that are attractive to both readers and advertisers, such as travel sections, or of introducing sections that may have limited reader appeal but a lot of associated advertising. The extent, and sometimes the content, of these sections depends on the advertising associated with it. Another strategy is to grow the advertorial content of a publication, and to develop special departments (sometimes combining editorial writers and advertising salespeople) to develop advertorial sections. Then there is the strategy of selling advertising around content such as personal finance, where advice columns are identified with a company selling personal finance products (Ueckermann 2005).

The growth of these strategies reflects strategic adjustments to a changing business and media environment. However, in a society that has expectations of the responsibilities of the media to citizens and to readers, media executives and journalists need to carefully consider the implications of modifications to the modus operandi of the media, in the same way that the media examine their role in a variety of other contexts. The South African media sector has had to reflect on its role during the apartheid era, through the 1997 Truth and Reconciliation Commission (TRC) hearings into the media in the apartheid era (TRC 1998), and on its role in representing race, through hearings by the South African Human Rights Commission (SAHRC) into racism in the media in 2000 (SAHRC 2000). Sanef has also raised a number of areas of concern for journalists in a variety of conferences and projects. In 2002, it sought to examine whether journalists were doing an adequate job of reporting news by funding a skills audit and by engaging in discussions with training institutions and media executives about ways in which journalists' skills could be improved (De Beer & Prince 2005).

Although, in discussion forums, there have been constant references to commercial factors as having an impact on journalistic work, there has not been a focused engagement with the question of the relationship with advertisers, with the exception of one or two areas of concern. Motoring journalists and their relationship with the automobile manufacturers recently came under the spotlight when *Beeld* motoring editor Marnus Hattingh raised issues of ethics with Sanef (Harber 2006). Sanef called on the South African Guild of Motoring Journalists to act on the allegations and investigate these practices.

> They referred to allegations of practices such as:
> - promises of quantities of editorial space promised in return for quantities of advertising
> - no clear distinction between editorial and advertising material

- questionable editorial, where motoring writers 'gloss over defects and pander to the manufacturers' desire for favourable publicity'. (Harber 2006)

The guild drew up a set of guidelines, but these were criticised for not dealing specifically with the issue of the relationship between advertising and editorial in motoring publications (Harber 2006). However, the incident does indicate a concern within the industry, even among specialist writers, about the blurring of advertorial and editorial.

Some media executives and commentators have argued that media companies are no different from baked bean producers (Crotty 2006) and should be allowed to get on with their core business of generating profits. Trevor Ncube, the owner of the *Mail & Guardian*, argued in one forum that no journalist should be employed who has not studied business and the Chinese wall that protected the newsroom from the demands of advertisers should be torn down (Harber 2004). It is true that a publication that is struggling to survive is in a difficult position when advertisers make demands and is more likely than lucrative media businesses to cave in under the pressure. However, as Crotty points out, purely commercial media, which operate in exactly the same way as any other business corporation, cannot expect the special status and freedoms they have in society.

Local media commentator Lynette Steenveld has argued that one of the media's functions in a democracy is specifically to develop citizenship:

> On one hand they provide informational and symbolic resources for citizenship; on the other, if their increased commercialisation and privatisation limits access to, and diversity of, these resources, then they cease to be social and politically useful institutions and therefore their status is not secure. (Steenveld 2004: 111)

It is the public interest that is invoked when the media are under threat of restriction from political interests or from legal provisions that govern other sectors of society. Media lawyer, Jacques Louw, cites judgments by South African courts that see the media's role in society as maintaining democracy, contributing to an exchange of ideas, and rooting out maladministration, dishonesty and corruption in government. He argues that '[t]he media play a crucial role in being vigilant by testing any attempt to restrict the public's right to receive information freely' (Louw 2005: 124). A media industry that cannot be depended on to perform these functions, and may itself be guilty of dishonesty, no longer has a rationale for its freedoms.

CHAPTER 4

Methodology

Broadly, this research aims to understand more about commercial pressures and their impact on media, and, by doing so, seeks to contribute to a debate about the role of South African print media in society. Specifically, we look at the practice of packaging editorial content with advertising – linking the two types of content – in order to sell more advertising, both in newspapers and magazines. The question of linked content comes under scrutiny because it is the interface of the two worlds of advertising and editorial, and shows shifts in the relationship between these two forces. There is a perception that such content is taking up increasingly more space in the mainstream news media and in quality magazines, and that it dominates most trade publications and niche magazines. Alongside is the fear of many journalists that linked content may not stay contained in certain sections, but is contaminating other parts of the publication. Some are concerned that we are moving towards a situation in which publications do not ever publish content without associated advertising, or that certain kinds of content may receive limited space because they do not attract advertising. In magazines, the relationship between advertising and editorial has always been more intertwined than the strict separation in news media. However, there have been concerns in specific areas, for example motoring publications, that the credibility of such publications may also be at risk.

For the purposes of this research, we have defined linked content as editorial content that is associated with advertising and sold to the advertiser as a package, and we have broadly categorised linked content into two types. First is the traditional advertorial package, where advertisers pay for articles to be written about their companies and products. These may appear under the title 'Surveys' or 'Advertising Feature' in the publications, and run next to display advertisements featuring the company or product. Second is the linking of editorial content to advertising through subject matter, for example, supplements such as travel or lifestyle, which then carry travel stories and travel advertising. Content linked on the basis of topic can be more and more narrowly defined, such as skincare features in women's magazines or valve features in engineering publications. This kind of linked content does not necessarily mean that the advertiser is 'king of content' in every case; some publications may decide that their readers would like certain kinds of content and then attempt to sell advertising around that content. However, when the supplement or feature section exists purely as a means to attract advertising, and there is no indication of reader interest, the balance has shifted away from editorial independence. It is significant to our inquiry to establish whether such sections are reader-driven or advertiser-driven.

The project was necessarily limited in scope. First, we looked at the prevalence and packaging of linked content in three publications: one financial magazine, one niche magazine and one daily newspaper. We chose the case study approach so that we could look closely at the commercial conditions in which a range of publications work, their business and journalistic practices, and the resulting content. This allowed us to look at the impact of strategies to attract advertising all along the chain of production, and, although the results cannot be generalised to all publications, they illustrate the kinds of issue and situation faced by publications, the kinds of choice they make to deal with them, and the effects of such choices on content.

To get a broader idea of how publications see their relationship with advertisers and how they try to manage that relationship, we interviewed media executives at five of the largest magazine companies in the country. They were asked about the conditions under which they operate, the strategies they use to attract advertising across all their titles, and whether there were codes for regulating advertising decisions for their publications. We also attempted to get their perceptions on whether there are changing trends in the sector. Apart from the analysis of their responses in this report, their recorded responses are available from the Media Observatory in the Department of Journalism at the University of the Witwatersrand.

Next we attempted to get a sense of how readers relate to advertorial and linked content by conducting four structured focus-group discussions with media students. As the groups were small and defined, it is not possible to generalise the results across the population. However, the qualitative nature of the research allowed us to observe how readers interact with a publication and its content, and to explore their responses to advertorial. Four groups of students currently engaged in studying the media or communications at the University of the Witwatersrand or at Tshwane University were asked to take part in structured focus group discussions.

Finally, we surveyed the codes and regulations relating to the media, to investigate whether there were any guidelines, ethical codes or regulations that regulate the relationship between advertising and editorial, and whether these are sufficiently relevant to current conditions in which media companies do business.

CHAPTER 5

Case studies

Finance Week

Finance Week is a weekly business magazine, established in 1979, which has recently been merged with *Finansies & Tegniek* to form *Finweek*. *Finweek* is now produced in both English and Afrikaans, and produces stories about finance and business for corporate executives, businesses owners, and government (just as its two predecessors did). In the years since its establishment, the title has gone through periodic changes of style and emphasis with regard to its content and operations, as part of ongoing attempts to make the magazine more profitable. The magazine now offers commentaries on various specific business matters, ranging from global and local economies and how they affect the ordinary man in the street to financial analysis and displays of keen understanding of market workings, both financial and otherwise. It also details the South African business environment.

The readership profile of the publication shows that that the title serves the upper end of the market, people in what SAARF has segmented as LSM 6–10, that is, people earning from R4 000 to R15 000 and over. The magazine boasted an audited circulation of 29 842 for the period of October to December 2005, and, in 2005, had a readership of 126 000, according to the All Media Products Survey (AMPS) ('Readership profile' 2006). The publication is now the top weekly business magazine in South Africa, followed by rival *Financial Mail*.

This research sought to examine some of the strategies used by *Finance Week*, before its merger, to attract advertising to the publication, and the implications of these strategies for content.[7] The period examined, the first half of 2003, was a time when the publication was once again trying to reposition itself, and the assumption was that, in this type of climate, a publication would be inclined to redefine its relationship with advertisers and to set up new and different strategies for attracting business. The research included interviews with executives at *Finance Week* and a content analysis of four editions of the magazine, from 5 May 2003 to 26 May 2003. The interviews were designed to discover what strategies were developed to attract advertising, to what extent these strategies included linking and packaging content and advertising together, how the advertising and editorial functions of the publication were separated or connected, and whether there were particular guidelines or principles for the placement of advertisements and advertorial copy. The content analysis mapped out the placement and quantity of advertising in different sections of the magazine, and looked for manifest links to editorial content.

---

7 This research depends heavily on original research done by the writer, Ndaba Dlamini, as part of the requirements for an Honours degree in Journalism and Media Studies at the University of the Witwatersrand.

Finance Week in context

Finance Week was bought from its original owners by Naspers in 1998, and became part of Media24, the print division of the company. In the same year, it was merged with *Finansies & Tegniek* for the first time. However, in September 2001, after research suggested product differentiation, a separation of *Finance Week* and *Finansies & Tegniek* was implemented because of the need for 'sustainability' (www.finweek.co.za).

In August 2001, a repositioning strategy was put into effect at the publication when Rikus Delport, the present editor of *Finweek*, took over at *Finance Week*. Editorial no longer focused on politics but more on financial issues and business. The change in content was basically a strategy to focus *Finance Week* on a particular aspect of the market and depart from 'extreme views' (Dlamini 2003) – which were political in nature – that tended to blur the business focus of the magazine. This position was reached after consultations with the editorial department, the managerial department and the executives when the publication began to suffer stiff competition from other magazines, especially from its rival business publication, *Financial Mail*. There was a particular refocus on the high end of the corporate investor market (LSM 8 and 9). *Finance Week* also moved its publication day from Wednesday to Monday.

The publication formulated an editorial policy in order to preserve the integrity of the magazine. Colleen Naude, deputy editor at *Finance Week*, said the publication had 'a firm policy of independence' and this independence was non-negotiable. The editorial policy of the magazine made it clear that editorial services provided by the publication were committed to a strict policy of editorial neutrality. It stressed that editorial content was strictly under the sole control of the *Finance Week* editors and that the magazine should carry editorial covering a wide range of subjects, all of which should be relevant to the target market of *Finance Week*.

Finance Week had a large editorial and staff complement, most of whom continue to work at *Finweek*. The editor was Rikus Delport, and Naude was his deputy editor. The associate editors were Tony Koenderman and Greta Steyn, with Sikonathi Mantshantsha being editorial assistant. Content was produced by a number of permanent journalists, columnists and 'contributors'. The advertising department is still headed by Trevor Louw, and has as sales executives Tian Liebenberg, John Hyman and Charles Duke.

Finance Week had a regular content line-up (much the same as *Finweek*). The publication averaged 72 pages and had a 'Cover Story', or front page story, and a 'News This Week' section that provided snippets of business news from the local and international scene. General business news could be found in the 'Openers' section, and there were specific companies that came under the spotlight in the 'Companies' section. 'Creating Wealth', a section that dealt with investment in the stock and unit trusts market, was also a regular, together with a section on advertising run by marketing commentator Koenderman.

There were also two kinds of special supplement. Naude said that the publication had one generic supplement, which focused on either agriculture or banking. A special advertising team – who only sell advertising space in the supplements – and the national advertising sales team liaised in coming up with ideas for supplements. The team would, for example, approach an agriculture company and inform them that the publication was producing a survey on agriculture, 'a survey that would serve your target market', said Naude. The editorial copy in these supplements would then be related to agriculture but would not be 'dependent on any advertisers advertising on the supplements', according to Naude.

Advertisers could place half-page advertisements in the supplement, said Naude, but there was no guarantee that *Finance Week* would also run editorial about or related to that particular company in that supplement. The advertisers did not pay for any editorial copy that appeared in the generic supplements.

The other type of section was the corporate survey or profile, which *Finance Week* 'branded carefully as "advertorial"'. Liebenberg said, 'This is when a company comes to us and says they would like to advertise in the magazine. They would say they would like to write the editorial copy but we would make sure that the word "Advertorial" is written at the top so that people can see that it is the advertiser's view or opinion'. The advertiser pays for the copy.

Liebenberg said it was imperative that editorial independence was maintained by a publication at all times, as this is what the credibility of a publication was based on.

> In certain instances, we compile a special feature or survey based on a specific industry that will be of interest to the readers. This creates an opportunity for an advertiser to position themselves as leaders in the industry and be closely associated with the editorial content of such a survey. The content of the editorial is never based on the amount of financial support we receive from a specific advertiser in terms of their adspend.

In a corporate survey, Standard Bank, for example, may have elected to write eight pages and clearly display a brand that distinguishes the survey from the editorial copy of *Finance Week*. According to Naude, Standard Bank would then pay for the copy or alternatively elect a *Finance Week* writer to produce copy for them. In such surveys, advertisers may have had advertisements facing such articles, but not in the main issue of *Finance Week*.

> Some advertisers sometimes insist their advertisements appear facing articles related to their company or in name or theme. However, *Finance Week* has a deliberate way to separate editorial from advertisements and there are a number of times when we have written critical articles about some of our clients and they threatened to pull out their advertisements for the whole year. Actually, most of our advertisers are big companies who book to advertise for the whole year.

In one case, Naude said, a critical article was written about one regular advertiser and the client pulled out all the advertisements for the whole year.

> Where we have written a critical article about a certain company, *Finance Week* has a policy of consulting and verifying with that particular company any information we want to publish. We ask them to point out any factual inaccuracies. Advertisers are allowed to correct any factual inaccuracies, not tamper with editorial.

There were a number of prime positions that an advertiser could request for their advertisement 'at an increased rate', such as the inside covers and back cover (but not the outside front cover). Naude observed that '[t]he magazine consists of different sections like Investment, Property, etc. An advertiser can request for their advertisement to appear in a specific section, that is, an investment company may request their ad to appear in the "Investment" section'.

The editorial department liaised with the advertising department and suggested topics for any surveys that may have been planned. Naude explained:

> We usually get someone with expertise in, for example, agriculture and they meet with the surveys team. But as far as 'natural advertising' (advertising that appears in the main issue) is concerned, the advertising team is very much on their own and is concerned with building up relationships with our major clients, the big advertising companies.

Liebenberg said that any company could submit editorial copy to the publication – whether they were advertisers or not. Copy and press releases were published based on the reader value they could add to the publication or level of interest, and not whether the company was a *Finance Week* advertiser or not.

The ratio of editorial to advertising varied in any issue of *Finance Week*. Like most niche publications, Naude said, *Finance Week* was also dependent on advertising for most of its revenue. Liebenberg concurred with Naude and said the average split between advertising and editorial content was usually a 30/70 split for the main body of the magazine and a 50/50 split for surveys. 'It is also important to realise that a reader (which is the actual product you are selling to an advertiser) buys a publication for its editorial content value and not because they will be able to see certain advertisements in the publication.' Liebenberg said that the average split for revenue was 70 per cent from advertising sales and 30 per cent from copy sales.

In terms of advertising, Liebenberg said that *Finance Week* offered potential advertisers a specific readership – a person with a specific income, which meant that he or she held the required spending power in order to spend money with the potential advertiser:

> Usually, this person would hold a position in the companies they work for and usually has a high level of influence in buying and decision-making. These attributes are then mapped out according to the 'identity' and characteristics of whom the advertiser would like to target. Should there be

synergy and compelling enough reason for the advertiser to advertise with the publication, the reasons for advertising are obvious. It is important to remember that you will have to do a thorough needs analysis prior to just trying to sell a potential advertiser into a publication. Is the readership that you are offering the right market in terms of who the advertiser is trying to reach?

Although, at that stage, *Finance Week* played second fiddle to *Financial Mail*, it offered a 'different readership' from that of the competition. Liebenberg explained:

> Although there is an overlap in the readership, both *Finance Week* and the competition can offer its readership's own uniquenesses. There are a lot of advertisers that will advertise in both publications in order to extend their reach to their target audience, and because both publications offer them a great vehicle to the average business person. For advertising a product aimed at a more specific reader, the advertiser then weighs up the pros and cons of the two magazines and advertises with the publication most suited to its requirements.

The operational relationship between the *Finance Week* advertising department and advertisers is 'solid'. Liebenberg said, 'From the above revenue split, it is evident that, without the advertisers, it would be close to impossible for a magazine to survive. We have dedicated teams that service and assist advertisers in the readership information they require.'

Content analysis of *Finance Week*

For the purposes of this study, four issues of *Finance Week* from the period of 5 May 2003 to 26 May 2003 were selected for study. The contents of the magazines were analysed to determine how many advertisements (full or half page) there were in each issue. Links between advertisements to editorial copy and the inverse were also looked at. This was split into links between the advertisement and the editorial content by name of the advertiser/company or story theme (whether the article dealt with company, investment, money market, finance or lifestyle news). The links between advertisements on the same or opposite page or elsewhere in the magazine, as well as stand-alone advertisements, were also analysed. The number of advertisements was also counted.

For the purposes of this study, letters to the editor and articles under the section 'News This Week' – snippets of local and international news – were left out. The cover story usually presented the most important news covered by the magazine. Generally, the theme of the cover story varied from issue to issue – it might have dealt with financial services, companies, or the money market, for instance. One of the regular sections that appeared and took up a large part of the magazine was the 'Companies' section. This section dealt with news about the operations, stock market dealings and financial standing of the companies under review. Only one advertorial marked as such was found in the issues under study.

The average percentages were calculated after counting and adding the number of linked advertisements or linked editorial content that appeared on the same or opposite page or elsewhere in the issues under study, divided by the total number of advertisements or editorial content in the four issues under study. To avoid duplication, for example, advertisements linked by name on the same or opposite page were not considered in the calculation of advertisements linked by theme on the same or opposite page.

Most of the advertisers were corporate banks such as Standard Bank, Nedbank and Absa, finance companies such as Sanlam, Allan Gray and Futuregrowth Unit Trust, as well as Telkom, Sasol and Eskom.

Liebenberg and Naude put the average split between advertisements and editorial content at 30/70. A look at the editions in the study indicated that the average split was 35/65. An analysis of the four issues to determine whether advertisements were linked to editorial content by name or theme indicated that advertisements linked by name on the same or opposite page averaged 9%, while advertisements linked by name elsewhere in the issues averaged 5%. On the other hand, advertisements linked to editorial content by theme on the same or opposite page averaged 19% and those linked by theme located elsewhere in the issues averaged 34%. Unlinked advertisements averaged 33%.

An analysis of editorial content linked to advertisements by name or theme indicated that an average of only 1% of stories were linked by name on the same or opposite page, while 6% of stories were linked by name to advertisements elsewhere in the issues. Editorial content linked to advertisements by theme on the same or opposite page averaged 3%. A huge number of stories, averaging 80%, were linked to advertisements by theme elsewhere in the issues. Unlinked stories averaged 10%.

The findings above indicate that *Finance Week* holds true to its policy of having little editorial–advertising linkage on the same or opposite page. However, since *Finance Week* is a niche magazine aimed at a niche audience, advertisers advertising in the title will tend to be linked by theme. Business magazines tend to attract corporate companies and banks, and this holds true with the ads found in *Finance Week*. The high percentage of linked advertisements in all issues under study reveals the high targeting nature of the magazine. Advertisers want an audience that has the right characteristics to buy their goods or services, and *Finance Week* seems to provide them with them with the right kind of atmosphere.

In the four issues under study, there were five surveys in total, and all advertisements that appeared in the surveys were linked to the editorial content, whether by name or theme. Advertisements linked to editorial content by name on the same or opposite page averaged 21% across all the surveys and those linked by name anywhere else in the issue constituted 18% of advertisements. Advertisements linked by theme on the same or opposite page averaged 29% and those that appeared elsewhere averaged 32%.

In the surveys, advertisers seem to have the freedom to choose where they would like to place their advertisements, judging by the high number of advertisements that appear next to related stories. Liebenberg says that this is also due to the working relationship between *Finance Week* and advertisers, where advertisers are approached and given a chance to advertise next to appropriate content. However, advertorial sections are signalled in particular ways in certain cases.

For example, in the issue of 26 May, in a corporate survey of Coris Capital (a financial service provider company), the logo of the company is displayed alongside the *Finance Week* logo on the first page of the survey to show that it's paid for. The logo shows that the editorial content in the survey was paid for by the company under review, unlike other surveys, which do not display any company logos and comprise several companies. However, there is no title above the section saying 'Survey' or 'Advertorial'.

On the other hand, a supplement on a theme, such as the 50-page golf supplement that appeared in the issue of 19 May, would produce editorial separately from advertising and there would be few links between copy and advertisements. The supplement had 16 advertisements, of which only six were linked by name or theme to editorial. The average advertising/editorial split is about 40/60, quite unprecedented for a supplement. The advertisements, however, are clearly targeted at the corporate clientele who play the sport. The companies comprise South African Airways, PriceWaterhouse Coopers, Sanlam, Jaguar, Medihelp Medical Scheme and Cell-C Business. The average percentage of unlinked advertisements stood at a high of 62% and unlinked stories stood at 67%. An unprecedented average percentage of 19% advertisements were linked by theme to stories that appear on the same or opposite page. There were no advertisements linked by name or theme to editorial, whether on the same or opposite page or anywhere else in the supplement.

Discussion

This research was conducted before *Finance Week* was merged with *Finansies & Tegniek* to form *Finweek*, which means that *Finance Week's* practices and strategies cannot automatically be assumed to take place in the current publication, even though there has been much continuity of staff and structures. However, the research does provide some interesting insights into the way in which a quality niche publication attempts to balance editorial credibility with the commercial enterprise of growing advertising.

The first strategy by the publication to preserve its editorial integrity was that there were very few advertisements linked by name to news stories on the same or opposite page, explicitly to protect the credibility of editorial for readers. However, there were links – by name or brand – between advertisements and editorial that were carried elsewhere in the publication. The high number of regular advertisers also seemed to play a role in the number of 'mentions' the advertisers enjoyed in any one issue. Advertisers such as Sanlam and Nedbank either had their directors, executives or managers quoted in stories or their corporate dealings were focused on.

However, this was the result of a niche publication that had readers, newsmakers and advertisers all coming out of the same pool.

Because *Finance Week* readers were highly educated people, Naude said they were more likely than other readers of general-interest publications to spot any advertiser intrusion in any story. That is why there was a deliberate effort to avoid any open advertiser spillover. For this reason, there was very little advertorial. Only one advertorial, branded as such, was found out of all the publications. According to Liebenberg, sceptical readers did not usually take seriously any editorial material branded 'advertorial', and most advertisers would rather use the survey section or supplements to place paid editorial. However, paid-for editorial produced for advertisers was still used in the survey sections.

Finance Week was clearly careful to guard its credibility with its readers, as they felt their readers would be alert to any blurring of advertising with editorial. However, the supplements and surveys appeared to give more leeway to advertisers and often did carry paid-for editorial content. This appears to indicate that *Finance Week* saw supplements and special sections as being exempt from the firm guidelines they set for the main body of the magazine, and supplements and surveys were handled by a separate team of advertising salespeople and writers. Further, it is not clear whether the supplements and special sections were generally developed to attract advertising or for reader interest, or whether those two elements were equally considered in the decision-making process.

Audio Video

Audio Video, which has been around since 1988, serves a readership of hi-fi and home theatre enthusiasts, audiophiles and the retail trade by reporting on electronic products. In the magazine's current glossy magazine format, it can be found in CNA, Exclusive Books, Spar stores, airport bookstores and Pick 'n Pay outlets. A total of 500 outlets display the magazine each month, usually alongside international titles and one other completely local title: *Multi Media*.[8] The magazine, sold and distributed through RNA, retails for R18, and shop sales almost double subscription sales. With a total readership of 22 000, each magazine is read by three different people and it counts among its assets a web site that averages 100 000 hits a month, as consumers trade second-hand equipment. A recent reader survey, printed in the June 2005 edition, indicates that readers are difficult to pin down. Answers to the survey indicated that 14% of readers are younger than 30. Some 35% are between 31 and 40 years old, 29% are between 41 and 50, and 22% are older than 51 years.

In terms of income, 31% earn more than R200 000 a year, while 35% earn between R200 000 and R100 000 each year. Some 84% of readers clearly purchase the magazine for guidance, as 84% intend investing in equipment in the next year,

---

8 Since the conclusion of this research, the magazine's competitor – *Multi Media* – has undertaken to reprint content from UK magazine, *What HiFi*. Thus, there is no longer a direct competitor to *Audio Video* as the content of the magazine is no longer focused on local, or locally available products.

while 94% upgrade equipment annually. Most important, 74% think that reading the magazine gives them an edge – as they pass on advice gleaned from the magazine. Looking at categories, 73% will spend in the mid-range category, and 22% in the high-end category. Some 93% of readers own a DVD player and rent over three titles a month; and buy at least two CDs a month. Over half of the magazine readers thought the publication was 'good' and 89% surf the web site. Unsurprisingly, 75% of readers used the Internet and 77% had a home PC, but only 15% had moved to MP3 players at the time of the survey.

Catering to a niche market with the type of spending power that many advertisers hope to lure, the magazine serves the top bracket of the LSM category – the most affluent readers. However, despite these credentials, it finds itself in a tightly contested market for adspend. Given this context, we asked what strategies were in place to attract advertising to the magazine and what the implications of those strategies were for editorial content and for readers. In addition, we asked how the magazine responded to competition for advertising, whether advertisers had the upper hand and, if so, what the magazine did to prevent them abusing their dominant position – causing spillover of marketing into editorial. We asked, finally, how the magazine maintained its editorial integrity.

The aim of this study was to answer these questions through a combination of interviews with two editorial executives and a content analysis that spanned a year. The interviews were aimed at eliciting information about day-to-day practices on the publication in producing editorial, making deals with advertisers and negotiating these two functions. Such information also provided a basis for the content analysis, in identifying advertising content that was not signalled, and in setting out the particular strategies that could have an effect on content. The content analysis was therefore based on what arose from the interviews. It involved close scrutiny for manifest links between advertisements and editorial in different sections of the magazine, as well as counting editorial content that had been paid for by an advertiser and not been signalled. It also looked for correlations between different types of editorial.

Audio Video in context

Audio Video is a magazine that specialises in news and reviews of audio and video equipment. It aims to provide information on equipment that would be relevant to the high-end user. Accordingly, the editorial policy of the magazine indicates that it aims to differentiate itself from its competitors by providing reviews that are as factual and unbiased as possible. This aim could be undermined by the situation in which the magazine finds itself. As in travel and motoring journalism, *Audio Video* relies on its advertisers to provide news on new products and products for review. Unlike a more general interest publication, it reports on the companies and products that are advertised in the magazine, a situation that is bound to create conflict at times.

The magazine has a small permanent staff and a flat hierarchy. Bob Pryers and Deon Schoeman each own half the magazine and perform different functions. There are an editorial assistant, a managing editor and an assistant editor. In addition, there are nine contributors who freelance for the magazine. All of these report to Pryers, as he is presently full time, while Schoeman also edits the *Top Car* banner and appears on the Super Sport programme of the same name. All other production processes, such as layout, are outsourced. There are no advertising salespeople; Bob Pryers deals with advertising. Sometimes an advertiser will express an interest in placing an advertisement when assistant editor Kopping meets with them for editorial reasons. Kopping will hand such leads over to Pryers.

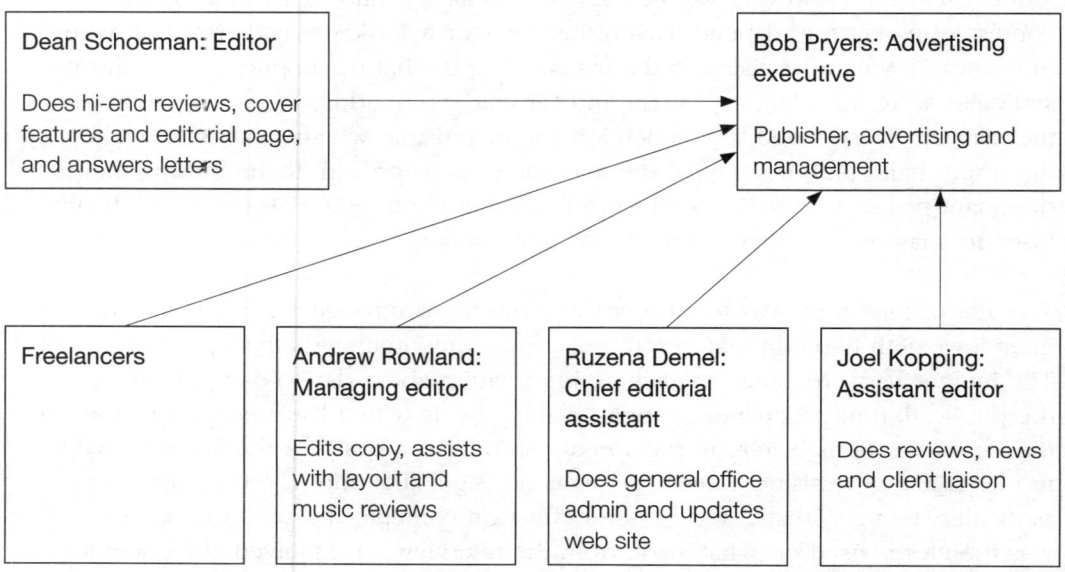

Figure 5.1 Audio Video: *Publishing, editorial, advertising and management structure*

Locally, *Audio Video* finds itself in a precarious position. Its only competitor is *Multi Media* magazine, which retails for slightly less than *Audio Video* does. But a plethora of international magazines is available, retailing for as much as R100, and these are fairly popular in South Africa presumably because products are often first launched internationally. Therefore, competition for adspend is not just split between *Audio Video* and *Multi Media*. Other magazines that feature 'boys' toys', such as the recently launched T3, compete in the same adspend arena. Pryers points out that products highlighted in international magazines and in T3 are often not available locally. Nevertheless, as names like LG® and Sony® are well-known brand names, general-interest local publications, too, are keen to get a share of adspend.

In addition, in 1997, when *Multi Media* arrived on the scene, effectively doubling the number of local magazines in this niche arena, it offered advertising rates at half those of *Audio Video*. Pryers has this to say: '*Multi Media* entered the market in 1997 and their initial approach was to influence the importer/distributor by giving them promises of unobtainable circulation and advertising rates, which were – at the time –

50% of our rate'. In addition, the entry of the new magazine placed constraints on news, as, according to Pryers, it sourced editorial directly from advertisers and lifted it almost word for word from other publications.

Pryers says that *Audio Video* survived the onslaught by maintaining low overheads – a characteristic that still persists in its small staff complement – and keeping advertising rates where they were. 'We continued to ride out the negative loss due to certain clients reducing or stopping advertising. Gradually, we grew our income and maintained editorial independence.'

As *Audio Video* specialises in news and reviews of audio and video equipment, its main focus is on products. A reader will often see a product up to three or four times in a single issue. It will make its entry as a news item, be reviewed and then possibly given away on the competition page. At some stage during this cycle, it will undoubtedly be advertised as well. Essentially, the magazine's readership – while including many audiophiles – also includes advertisers. Theoretically, if displeased, they can withhold a product for review, and this can only be to the magazine's disadvantage as it does not have the resources to buy products for review. The fact that advertisers hold sway does not seem to be in doubt; a look at the magazine's income ratio over the last financial year shows a disproportionate income split, giving the advertisers some kind of power – real or otherwise.

Figure 5.2 Audio Video: *Income streams as a percentage of total income*

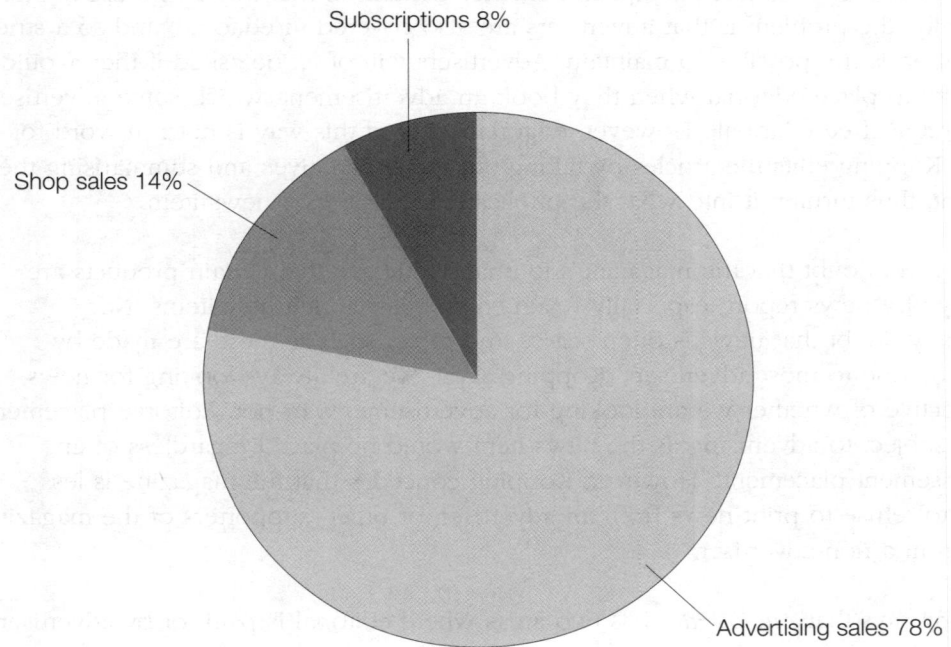

In addition, each article is factually cleared by the advertiser sponsoring the piece of equipment; in other words, the article is sent to the advertiser before being printed. There have only been two instances in which, as assistant editor Joel Kopping reports, reviews that have displeased advertisers have been suppressed. In both, the magazine could not afford to alienate a powerful source of revenue.

> We don't pull reviews as a matter of course. In the time I've been at the magazine, there have been two of my reviews that have been dropped. The first one was Kef speakers and my review was quite different to a UK review, and not quite as complimentary. What happened was that the distributor faxed through a copy of the UK review and, as I was not prepared to change what I said about the speaker, the distributor requested that the review not be published.

The magazine, says Kopping, complied because the distributor was a good advertiser. In the second instance, however, the decision was moot, as the distributor had – on the strength of the negative review and a lack of support from the US manufacturer – decided not to supply the speakers to the South African market. Generally, however, copy is returned unchanged unless the magazine has erred in a factual statement. Some advertisers do try to exert their influence beyond just the tactic of flexing power. Kopping tells of an instance in which an advertiser said, 'I know how things work and we will look after you', when handing in a review item. Kopping's response was to hand over the piece of equipment for review to editor Schoeman.

Nevertheless, a deliberate attempt to influence content in this way is not usual. More generally, the problem is that advertisers are also covered in editorial, and so a strict separation is not possible to maintain. Advertisers will often be asked if they would also like to place editorial when they book an advertisement, which some advertisers interpret as 'free editorial'. However, editorial sourced this way is not run word for word; Kopping edits the articles by taking out the superlatives and summarising the content, thus turning it into what the publication considers a news item.

There is no doubt that the magazine's journalists believe that certain products are worthy of a news report, especially when companies launch new items. Nor is there any doubt that news is often scarce and offers such as these are made by the magazine to most advertisers. Kopping says: 'We are always looking for news, irrespective of whether we are looking for advertisements or not. Editorial placement is not subject to advertising as the news item would be placed regardless of an advertisement placement.' However, Kopping concedes that the magazine is less likely to refuse to print news from an advertiser, or other 'supporters of the magazine' than from a non-advertiser.

Kopping says that *Audio Video* has two areas where editorial is paid for by advertisers and this is not signalled. The front page is sold; in other words, advertisers can pay to have their product pictured on the front cover. Kopping points out that this is a valuable source of revenue, as this means eleven front pages are sold. There is also a section called 'Spotlights', in which the copy has been provided by advertisers, or their representatives, who have paid for the space. This is not signalled, and this section does not appear in every edition. A 'Spotlight', which is usually two full pages of text and pictures, is the same cost as a full-page colour advert, both of which are half that of a cover. While neither the front page nor the 'Spotlight' is flagged as advertorial, Kopping argues that products would not make it onto these pages unless they were relevant to readers.

Content analysis of *Audio Video*

For the purposes of this research, 11 issues spanning a one-year period were analysed to determine links between editorial and advertisements. The content was analysed to determine how many advertisements there were in each issue (full, half and quarter page). Then we looked for manifest links between advertisements and editorial. An advertisement could be linked to an article in two ways: either through the product brand (for example, advertising for a Sony® product would be counted as linked to a news report if the report featured a Sony® product) or through a distributor that may import a range of products. We noted whether advertisements were linked to reports on the same page, on an 'overleaf' page, or elsewhere in the magazine. Also looked at under this category was paid-for editorial that was not signalled, such as covers. (All covers in the sample were paid for by an advertiser.) This determined the number of times that an advertisement was linked to an editorial, and in what sections this was happening. Next we examined editorial, looking for links to advertisements. Once again, we looked at links through brand mentions or distributor mentions. We also looked at what kinds of editorial – such as reviews or news items – were linked to advertising and whether certain editorial items were linked to other editorial. This allowed us to see how much editorial was not linked to advertising at all, and whether certain products, brands and companies were getting multiple mentions.

Audio Video, on average, is 72 pages in length and has – on average – one-and-a-half pages of competitions, 10 pages of CD/DVD/LP reviews, one column, 25 pages of reviews and seven pages of news. Some 25-odd pages are given to advertising, an advertisement ratio of about 40%. Letters take up about two pages and editorial comment one page, and the contents list takes up another page. News items are short, 150-word pieces that are essentially edited from press releases and, as such, are not by-lined. Product reviews are between 350 words and 1 200 words, depending on the category. Here we find 'Impressions', 'Focuses', 'Features' and 'Spotlights'. (As determined by the interviews, 'Spotlights' are reports that are sold and not marked as such.)

Pryers says that the average split between advertising and editorial content is 55/45; however, a look at the magazines in the period under review indicates that advertising takes up 42% of total page count. A look at advertisements to determine whether they are generally linked to editorial content in the same issue indicates that 67% are stand-alone with no link to content. One per cent are linked to editorial, either through mention of a brand name, such as LG® or Sony®, or a distributor on the same page, while those linked overleaf are too small to bear mentioning. Six per cent of editorial copy is sold, such as copy that is advertorial but not marked as such. Brand advertisers will have 6% of all their advertisements linked to editorial elsewhere in the magazine, while distributors more than double this figure at 19%. This means that some 67% of advertising is placed irrespective of whether there is editorial mentioning their brands or business, while 19% of advertisements are linked elsewhere through another reference to a distributor, and 6% through another mention to the same brand in editorial. Looking at links on the same page, both brands and distributors are likely to be linked to an advert on the same page 1% of the time.

Figure 5.3 Audio Video: *Advertising/editorial spillover*

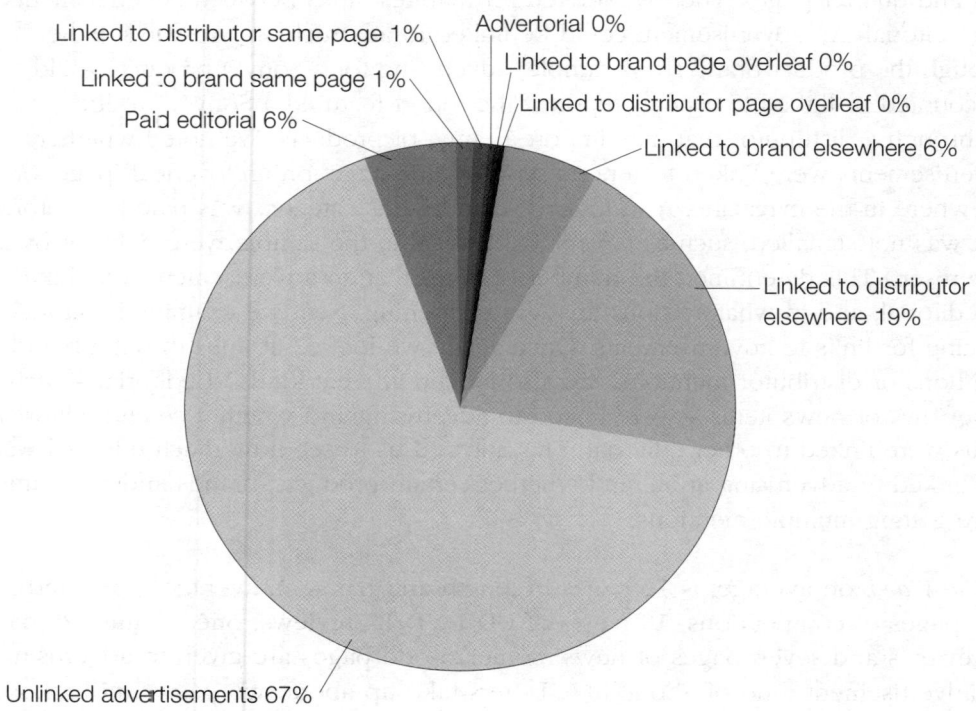

With news content, it is completely the opposite. Of the news content, some 80% is likely to be linked to advertising in some way. An interesting pattern that emerged during the interviews and content analysis, which was different from patterns in other publications examined, was the spread of stories in different sections about one product, and so this was analysed further in the content analysis. The chart in Figure 5.4 shows that it is more likely that repetitions of either the brand name or the distributor will occur in the news section. In other words, a distributor or brand company is more likely to have multiple mentions in news items than it is in reviews or advertisements. The least likely scenario, as seen from the chart, is that news items would have a linked advertisement on either the same or the adjoining page.

There is a close correlation between multiple news items and advertisements across the magazine. For example, a reader reading a news item may also see the same 'brand' in a review. Kopping suggests that this is often the result of *Audio Video* contacting a company for information for editorial. This is likely to result in the client supplying several categories of information at once, such as several news items, an advertisement and a product to review. This is unplanned by the magazine and depends on product launches or visits, and it often results in disproportionate coverage of a brand or distributor in an edition, as one name will have more coverage than another. Kopping adds that, when many products are launched at the same time, the magazine spreads these over a three- or four-month period to avoid 'brand fatigue'. But an in-depth look at which companies receive more coverage later will reveal that these are often the smaller companies; they are distributors rather than big brand companies.

Figure 5.4 Audio Video: *Percentage of linked news content*

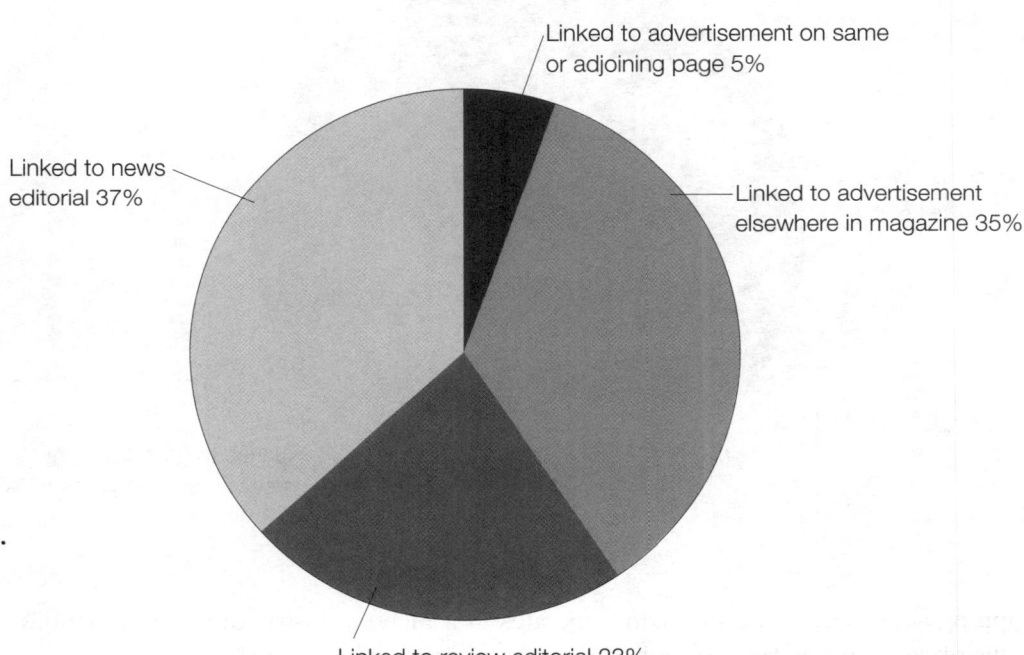

Points scored for the chart were awarded on the basis of a brand or distributor having multiple entries in the magazine. In other words, those who had only a single piece of editorial were not counted for the purposes of the chart. The aim was to determine where it was most likely that repeat naming would occur. In many instances this resulted in duplications, as, for example, some advertisers would have several advertisements for one editorial. However, the aim behind the methodology was to indicate how many brands that were featured in the news section would also appear in advertising and other editorial sections.

A look at reviews undertaken with the same methodology as used in the graph in Figure 5.4 indicates that either those who advertise are more likely to get a review included in the magazine, or companies that send products in for review are also likely to place an advertisement. Kopping says that, should a distributor or a brand owner have a product review in the magazine, they are more likely to advertise. Some 96% of review content is likely to be linked somewhere else in the magazine, 57% of the time to an advertisement in the magazine, 14% of the time to another review and 21% of the time to a news editorial through the distributor or brand name.

Figure 5.5 Audio Video: *Percentage of linked review content*

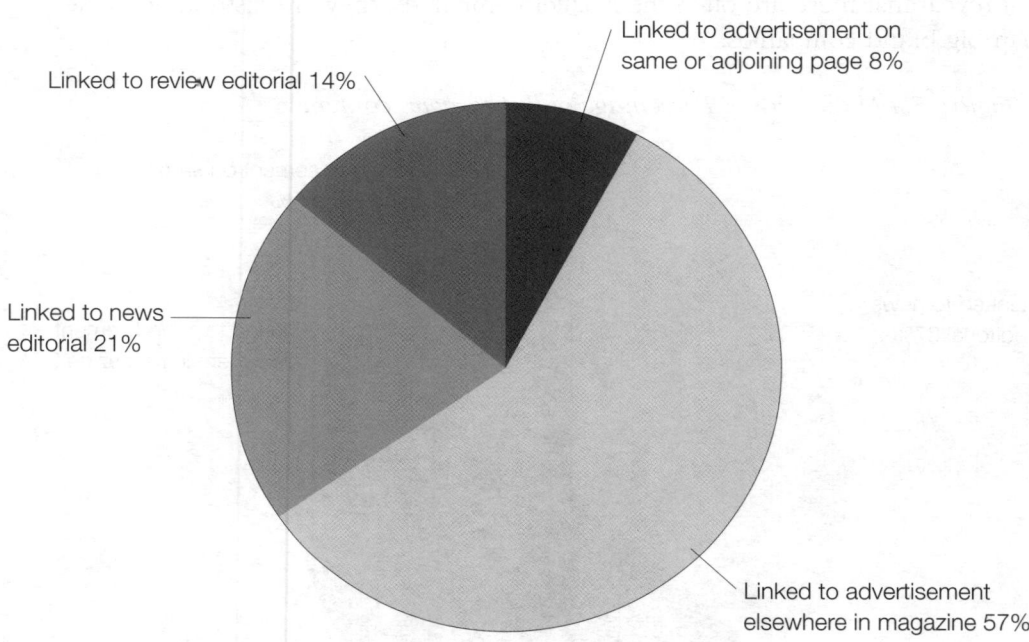

Kopping says that, as the magazine operates in a niche industry, there are a handful of distributors in the mid- to high-end of the industry and, as such, there is a core group of regular advertisers and those who often send products for review and as news items. Companies that are more proactive and actively submit items for publication as news or for review are more likely to have repeat mentions. Moreover, as there is less hierarchy in smaller companies, these are more likely to have more mentions as they are more approachable. Kopping cites examples such as HFX Systems, Jade Services, Balanced Audio, Mandarin and Audio Tronic as companies that are approachable. These companies regularly provide news and products to the magazine, which aids the magazine and gets mentions for the companies.

Product releases that are released in batches – usually by brand owners – will also garner more space. However, this ties in with a global marketing strategy and is not indicative of the relationship with the magazine. This is borne out in the content analysis, which shows that the smaller distributors are more likely to average three mentions in an issue, compared to brand owners who submit news or products in fits and starts. It is clear from the interviews and content analysis, then, that companies play a large role in setting the content agenda for the magazine, but whether this is simply because they are advertisers or because they are proactive in marketing (advertising being only one mechanism used to promote their products) is not entirely clear.

On each item, information is provided – such as contact details – and it is often difficult, if not impossible, to distinguish paid-for editorial from unpaid editorial. Sometimes, the presence of a logo can signal advertorial; however, all pages are laid out in the magazine's style and look like standard editorial. One item that looked like paid-for content – when it was not – was a 40-year birthday celebration that had a particular background. From time to time, a feature will appear that bears an advertiser's logo, yet looks otherwise like editorial. Also from time to time, a non-advertising-related review will appear, such as a three-issue look at practical speaker information. Kopping says the magazine is considering this as a useful service to readers that does not rely on advertisers' input, and it may run more informative features in future.

The first-known entry of advertorial was in September this year, with a one-page piece that clearly stood out and was marked as advertorial. Pryers explains that this is indeed rare. The advertisers did not – at the time – have a print budget, and the public relations company motivated for an advertorial. Generally, he says, a review or news item would be run even though there was no advertising associated with it, but in this way at least the magazine received adspend.

Discussion

There can be no argument about the fact that that there are direct correlations between advertisements and editorial in *Audio Video* magazine. The research has found that 96% of review content is likely to be linked somewhere else in the magazine, 57% of the time to an advertisement in the same edition. By the same token, some 80% of news content is likely to be linked in some way either to an advertisement or another news item, or to a review. But a distributor or a brand-owning company is more likely to have multiple news items (submitted editorial) than to have multiple reviews or links with advertisements. However, the fact that there is a close correlation between multiple news items and advertisements across the magazine, at 35%, cannot be ignored. Add to this the fact that some 6% of content is paid for and not indicated as anything other than content, and the magazine seems to be on precarious ethical turf.

In addition, advertisers certainly know that they hold the balance of power. This can clearly be seen in the way that advertisers presume that editorial is free if an advertisement is booked – this is despite editorial submission being open to all distributors and no absolute guarantees being made. In addition, the magazine has suppressed reviews lest the advertiser take its spending elsewhere, despite this being only two instances out of about 770 in a five-year-period – an incidence of 0.26%.

However, the figures do show that more than two-thirds of advertisements are independent of any editorial content, which indicates that the simple fact of taking an advertisement does not guarantee an editorial mention. Indeed, it is editorial that is the more likely to be linked to another type of content. This suggests that the magazine reflects the marketing practices of its core advertisers, who are likely to submit news, advertisements and a product for review simultaneously on a regular basis. In addition, as it is the smaller companies that show these tendencies most frequently, this indicates good business sense rather than an attempt to exercise power.

This, however, does not detract from the grey area practices of seeming to offer free editorial with bookings, suppressing reviews that are unfavourable (even if on very rare occasions) and allowing advertisers to peruse reviews. Add to this the practice of running paid-for editorial in a style no different from the rest of the magazine and selling the front page, and readers are bound to wonder about credibility. Moreover, the fact that advertisers provide the product to be reviewed is problematic.

In its favour, the magazine does indeed follow principles of disclosure as far as possible and has recently taken to a second opinion on contentious reviews. Moreover, equipment owned by a reviewer that could be the subject of a review is loaned to another reviewer. Despite the fact-checking process, most reviews are unchanged and the magazine maintains that it manages to keep its editorial integrity in a difficult situation. However, as the magazine presents itself as a specialist publication that provides its readers with information they need to make purchases, it is clearly important that editorial content should maintain the maximum credibility. Much as in the motoring fraternity, writers and publications that report on and review products should consider a set of guidelines to protect both the consumer and their own credibility.

The Independent Group Special Projects Division

Independent Newspapers is one of the largest newspaper groups in South Africa, publishing 11 daily and weekly papers, mostly concentrated around the three metropolitan areas of Johannesburg, Cape Town and Durban. In the early 1990s, the Irish-based multinational Independent Newspapers, owned by Tony O'Reilly, bought a 31 per cent stake in the Argus Company, already a major player in the South African media industry. Independent Newspapers gradually expanded, buying and consolidating various titles. Today the company reaches more than four million people in combined circulation figures, and controls more than 39 per cent of South African print media, in terms of titles and circulation (South Africa Info 2006).

The Independent stable includes the daily papers *Cape Argus*, *Cape Times*, *Daily News*, *Diamond Fields Advertiser*, *Isolezwe*, *The Mercury*, and *Pretoria News*; and weeklies

The Post, Sunday Independent, and *Sunday Tribune* (Independent Online 2006). *The Star*, published in Johannesburg, is one of the most important titles in the group, with the largest circulation and readership amongst the Independent dailies. It averages 170 000 copies in daily sales, reaching an average daily readership of around 600 000 (South Africa Info 2006).

But *The Star* lost its position as South Africa's largest-selling daily when the tabloid newcomer *The Sun* expanded its circulation to more than 400 000. *The Star* also faces stiff competition for advertising revenue. With new media titles and outlets having come into the market, and the move by advertisers from mass audiences to segmented audiences, publishers of general-interest newspapers have been forced to develop new strategies that will generate new revenue streams, keep advertisers happy, and reach a targeted audience.

In the print industry, advertising surveys have long been one means by which newspapers generate revenue. These could be sections based on a particular theme, such as home security during the holidays, which attracts advertisers in a related industry who want their products or services to be associated with that kind of content, or sections where both the editorial reports and the advertising are paid for by advertisers. This kind of content is called advertorial and is usually signalled.

Recent trends in the South African media suggest that these special feature and survey sections are being increased and developed to attract more advertising revenue, and this forms part of the strategic planning of print companies. In this research we sought to investigate whether this was indeed the case at the Independent Group, and, if so, to examine the business and editorial practices associated with producing surveys at their newspapers, what regulates the relationship between editorial and advertising, and the potential implications for content and readers. The research consisted of interviews with key personnel at the Independent Group Special Projects Division, as well as a content analysis of *The Star* over the month of March 2005, in which the frequency and content of special features sections was examined.

The Special Projects Division

Carrying surveys is not an innovation of the Independent Group, as they had previously been carried in the Argus Company newspapers. However, in 1990, a permanent division was created to develop and drive this strategy, catering for all publications in the group. This division is known as the Special Projects Division. Its main function is actively to seek out potential advertisers who want to place their advertising in the right kind of editorial environment for their products. These sections are run across all the publications in the group, depending on the type, theme and target of the content. In this way they increase audience reach for the advertiser at a limited additional cost to the division, which produces the copy and sells the advertisements.

History and context

The Special Projects Division was established in January 1990 when Terry Meyer, now managing editor of the division, joined the Independent Group and proposed the idea. It became the group's first concerted foray into turning sporadic surveys into regular features in its papers.

The Special Projects Division falls under the commercial arm of the Independent Group, but is separate from the marketing department that deals with other regular adverts and classifieds, and is separate from the editorial departments. It generates a substantial amount of revenue, counted separately from that brought in through the normal advertisements and classifieds carried by the various papers in the group. Meyer would not say how much revenue and what proportion of advertising revenue Special Projects brings in. However, advertisers pay the same rate for this position as they do for other advertisements in the regular section of the paper. Considering that adverts take 60 per cent of the pages, and these features take a double spread most of the time, it can be said that the feature does generate a substantial amount of revenue for the group.

The division is able to generate this amount of revenue by coming up with subjects or themes that advertisers may find appealing and decide to be linked to. Terry Meyer describes the division as 'a sort of hybrid between editorial and advertorial':

> We get the editorial focus, and then we ask people to support it by advertising. We do this by sending a marketing letter, which is a synopsis of the content of the subject we would be covering editorially. We give this [letter] to a team of sales people who then go out to the market and research the right sort of people who would support that survey, and when they get sufficient advertising, we run with the focus.

He says the topics for the sections are decided either by trends in society or news-making headlines.

> We look at the marketplace; sometimes we look at our own newspaper, and other media. We would look and see what the current trend is. For example, like tomorrow, we have car-free day throughout the country, organised by the Department of Transport – we look at something like that and say let's write about car-free day. We say let's go out and look for people who might support us as advertisers – that's essentially what we do.

Meyer says about 200 to 300 special features are done per year, which means a special feature appears at least three or four times per week, taking from two to four pages. They appear in various publications, depending on the theme and target. For example, if the section is business related, it goes into *Business Report*, which is carried in all the group's main papers. If it is a consumer theme, it goes to the main body of the various newspapers, also depending on whether it is regional or national. Generally, freelancers are used to produce the copy.

Meyer maintains that there is some editorial independence: 'Yes, the advertisers do have some influence over the content, but the paper still maintains strict editorial independence'. However, he also says the following:

> But if, for example, someone has a particularly good news story, and we are covering a particular subject and the company phones us and says: 'Well, I have a particularly interesting and newsworthy subject, would you be able to publish it?' I'll say submit it and let's evaluate the merits of its newsworthiness, and then the journalist will look at it and rewrite it in a way that is readable and not biased particularly towards any company, so … it's evaluated on its newsworthiness.

Meyer says that publications are increasingly resorting to this strategy as a means of survival:

> I think as publications, especially smaller print publications, have battled to survive, they have gone more and more into this field, and even to advertorials, which they have never done before. You look at magazines now; they carry many advertorial pages which were taboo years ago; now they do it as a survival strategy.

Editorial content

Lorain Tulleken is one of the main writers for the sections produced by Special Projects. However, her job differs from that of a journalist in the news section as one of her responsibilities is to convince the advertisers of the necessity to be associated with a particular survey or feature. After the section is sold, she will write the editorial for it. She explains:

> You need a mix of 60% advertisement, and 40% editorial on a page for the venture to be viable. For special projects, if the balance is below 60% advertising, they will sometimes go to 50%, but it hits their profits very badly, and if they have below 50%, they will sometimes cancel the whole thing.

She says the topics for the features depend on trends and how they can be sold to the advertisers. Recently, Trevor Manuel commented that companies were not doing enough on broad-based black economic empowerment. Tulleken, setting out this theme in order to sell the idea to the advertisers, wrote: 'There must be companies out there that are moving fast enough. Why not tell the finance minister by buying advertising? … I'll write the copy'.

Even though Tulleken says she does most of the research for the features, she says that a lot of her material comes from the advertisers. 'I deal with a lot of professional public relations people; I get them to help with the information, so our turnaround time is very quick.' She adds that very often the companies that are advertising will buy extra copies of the newspaper, and use it for extra marketing.

In her role as the journalist writing the features, she says her challenge is to add credibility to the advertising features, because it can be tempting just to go with the copy provided by the advertisers, and sometimes it is impossible not to.

> But the reality is – and we would not say this too loudly – if I have two newsworthy stories, good news stories, and the one features an advertiser, and the other does not, which one am I going to print? The advertising one, of course, but it has to be newsworthy. It's also a fine balance, depending on the size of the business and other things that we take into consideration.

She says that her job is to try to make the readers forget that what they are reading is advertorial. 'The trick of special projects is to make it look like it is part of the newspaper,' because the nature of communications has changed tremendously and people are more perceptive and media-savvy. Tulleken rejects the notion that such practices can hamper the credibility of the newspaper. 'It cannot damage the credibility of the paper, because special projects do not pretend to be anything else. As it is clearly stated there, it provides a service to people.'

The bulk of advertorial on these pages comes from the business and finance sectors – big and small – as well as various governmental and non-governmental agencies, especially when they are running a particular campaign. It seems government agencies are increasingly using this means because it gives credibility to their communication with the public. Tulleken says, 'Every now and again, government will buy a whole page ... We are only involved in editing into our style, and into readable language and format'. She says the credibility factor is more important for government than it is for business:

> They [government] do this because they want control over the content. The important thing to look at here is ten, fifteen years ago, the credibility factor would have been much more important than it is right now, because readers are much more sophisticated. They recognise immediately what the papers are saying, so you are not fooling the public. People are much more educated in terms of branding, and advertorial.

Content analysis of *The Star*

The content analysis for this case study differed from the content analyses conducted on the magazines, as we were looking at a particular variation of linked advertising and editorial content, and the structure of Special Projects and the environment into which they fit differs from those of the magazines. The interface between the publication and the section arose as a potential issue during the research, so we included a focus on it in the examination of content. It was also important for the research to consider the themes (and thus the kinds of story being added to the newspapers) that were being proposed to advertisers, as this is where the impact is on editorial content.

We chose to look at *The Star* because it is the flagship publication of the Independent Group. First, we looked at the frequency with which the advertising features of the Special Projects Division appeared, and then we mapped the various themes, trends and advertisers. The content analysis was also designed to give us an idea of the number of advertisements that the features pulled in a given period and, in so doing, an estimate of the percentage of revenue they generated. The analysis also looked at news in the main sections of the paper to see whether there was any topic related to the stories covered in the Special Projects features, and how the coverage of this might potentially differ from one section to the other.

Special Projects features are usually placed in the second inside section of *The Star*, or the *Business Report* section. The inside section carries 'Verve' (a feature section), the leader page, opinion and analysis, commentaries and sports columns of the paper. When this section carries Special Projects features, they most often appear after the opinion pages.

Business Report is an insert that is carried by all the main papers of the group, according to Terry Meyer. Printed separately, it carries the business, finance and company news of all the papers of the group. It has a separate editorial team from the individual newspapers. Stories published in this section are mostly business related.

In March 2005, a total of 19 different advertising features were carried in 15 editions of *The Star*. Eleven of the features were published in the second section, while eight were carried by *Business Report*, taking 24 out of a total of 176 pages of the 15 issues that they were published in (about 13 per cent of all pages). Linked to these 19 features were 64 advertisements of various sizes. All advertisers on the pages were linked by theme to the subject of the feature. In most cases, the advertisers were directly mentioned or featured in the articles, and some of the articles were dedicated to them, focusing entirely on them, and quoting their representatives exclusively.

It was noted that more than half of the features published in the inside section of the paper came from government departments, government agencies or parastatals. For example, the edition of 8 March carried a focus on women and environment. This covered a whole page with various articles on the theme of women and development, focusing on the Women and Environment Conference held during the same week in Johannesburg, organised by the Department of Environmental Affairs and Tourism. The main article focused on the speech delivered at the conference by the deputy minister for environment and tourism, Rejoice Mabudafhasi. Other articles looked at various issues raised during the conference.

On 17 and 18 March, the paper carried the Department of Justice's 'Justice for All' campaign, an awareness campaign promoting the *Equality and Prevention of Unfair Discrimination Act*. The main article featured explanations of the act, quoting the deputy minister of the department, and featuring his picture prominently.

Different communications and ad agencies manage the sales of advertisements on these pages. The in-house marketing team is not involved, as the person or firm in charge of advertisements for a particular theme or issue is clearly stated below the by-line of the writer at the top right-hand corner.

The features are sometimes called 'Retail Feature' when the focus is on one company or product, and 'Corporate Feature' when the focus is on corporate structures or organisations. The different headings do not mean any difference in the way the features are presented; they all have the same layout and design.

Table 5.1 Breakdown of advertisement features carried in The Star, *March 2005*

(a) Verve

Date	Theme	Number of pages
Wednesday 2 March	Affordable banking	1
Tuesday 8 March	Women and the environment	1
Thursday 10 March	The changing face of the JHB CBD	2
Thursday 17 March	Justice for all	1
Thursday 18 March	Justice for all	1
Thursday 18 March	Lock up for Easter	1
Thursday 23 March	National Water Week	2
Thursday 23 March	Johannesburg housing company	1
Friday 24 March	Modern photography	2
Thursday 31 March	Fourways focus	1
Thursday 31 March	Take a Girl Child to School Day	1

(b) Business Report

Date	Theme	Number of pages
Friday 4 March	Paper, print, packaging	2
Wednesday 9 March	Corporate social investment	1
Thursday 10 March	Property leasing – business properties	1
Monday 14 March	Medical health – alternative therapy	1
Wednesday 23 March	Colour copiers and printers	1
Wednesday 30 March	Collective investment	2
Thursday 31 March	Venture capital	1
Thursday 31 March	JSE sponsors	1

The research found two examples of coverage of the same themes by the Special Projects pages and the news pages of *The Star*. On 10 March, the second section of *The Star* carried a focus on the changing face of the Johannesburg CBD, and, on 23 March, a focus on the Johannesburg Housing Company. This carried various reports on initiatives made by the city to improve habitat, and to offer low-cost housing, while improving sanitation and clearing slums and slumlords in the city centre, making it a safe place. The 10 March feature said:

> … Johannesburg Inner City is a major economic generator in South Africa providing approximately 12% of national employment, with over one million people living, working and playing in the inner city … (Special Projects reporter 2005: 15)

The article went on to paint a positive picture of the regeneration of the Johannesburg Inner City and the creation of an Inner-city Tourism Association to drive this process. Advertising prominently on the page were the City of Johannesburg and other businesses located in the inner city.

This contrasted starkly with a page-one story in *The Star* a few weeks before, on 5 February, entitled 'Slumlords invade Johannesburg'. The article read as follows:

> Slumlords have conquered large chunks of Johannesburg, 'hijacking' houses and blocks of flats from their legitimate owners … As these areas are turned into vast slums occupied by tens of thousands of people living in appalling conditions, the City of Johannesburg is unable to evict illegal tenants and recoup unpaid water, electricity and rates bills. The slum belt includes the high-rise zones of the city itself, but has spread to the residential areas on the periphery, including Bertrams, Malvern, Jeppestown and Troyeville. There are also cases where slumlords are operating in Houghton. (Gallagher 2005: 1)

In another example, when Finance Minister Trevor Manuel came out strongly against empowerment companies for not being broad-based enough, the news was reported and analysed in the news pages and opinions and views were carried by a wide range of parties (including those slated by the minister). This was in keeping with the journalistic practice of offering fair and balanced information to the public. But, in preparing a Special Projects focus on the issue, Tulleken wrote to advertisers telling them that there must be some of them that were doing something on the black empowerment front. She encouraged them to take advertisements in the paper, and said she'd write the editorial copy, telling the minister that he was not entirely right, but without giving either the minister or other independent bodies the right to respond. This indicates that the editorial stance on such issues, usually set by the editor or a senior editorial team, does not extend to the Special Projects content.

Codes

Unlike most other companies, *The Star* has an ethical code that explicitly addresses the relationship between advertisers and the newspaper in what it calls 'surveys', 'advertising features' and 'service features' (Independent Newspapers 2006). A core principle for all material related to advertising is that 'readers should be left in no doubt about the source of copy. If material has been provided by advertisers or other sources outside *The Star*, this should be clearly stated' (2006). Surveys and service features operate according to many of the codes of the newsroom, with journalists specifically advised that they may not liaise with sales representatives and advertisers on editorial content, although they may contact advertisers for information that they feel is necessary to the stories they are writing. The guidelines for what the code calls 'advertising features' allow the use of advertorial and the involvement of advertisers in the production of the section, but state specifically that 'these products must be clearly labelled ADVERTISING FEATURES. In addition, readers should be told that information was obtained from the client/clients' (2006).

The sections under Special Projects are not addressed in the codes. Although these are not exactly advertising features, they do not operate like surveys either, which is probably what Meyer means by a 'hybrid between advertorial and editorial'. It is clear, though, that they do carry information supplied by the advertisers, especially in the case of government, and that this is not signalled in accordance with what *The Star's* own codes require.

Discussion

The aim of this research was to investigate, by looking at the Independent Group Special Projects Division, a perceived trend in media companies of refining, developing and actively promoting advertorial and survey sections, how such a strategy would work in practice, and to investigate the potential impact on editorial content, on readers and on credibility. On the first question – the development of sections with linked editorial and advertising content – there can be no doubt that the Independent Group set up the Special Projects Division to proactively develop 'a mix between advertorial and editorial' to attract a range of advertisers to the publication. Meyer also indicated that this was happening across the print industry, which bears out other evidence that this has become an important way of doing business for media groups.

Given that the traditional way of doing business in publications has been to separate editorial and advertising, of interest here is the development of a new and additional practice, which continues to keep the mainstream editorial and advertising apart, but which has a third arm for special sections. This division of the media business develops and blurs advertising, public relations and journalism in an effort to attract more advertising revenue and also to produce readable content. It then raises the question of how the interests of readers are safeguarded and accommodated in such sections, and the potential impact of such sections on main body editorial.

As Tulleken said, working with professional public relations people from the advertisers means that there is a quick turnover of copy because she is supplied most of the time with the content. Though she holds that the articles have to attain certain journalistic standards, she admits that they are not critical and are sometimes biased towards the advertisers. Even though she tries to give the articles credibility, the fact that most of the material she works with comes from the advertisers, and that they pay for it, indicates that the advertising and public relations function of the section takes precedence.

There is also the issue of how the topics for the sections are conceived. Both Meyer and Tulleken talk about 'trends in society' as the factor that influences the ideas the division comes up with. However, a look at the sections in March shows that some of the themes were generated by advertiser imperatives, especially when the advertiser was government (new policies, etc.). This does not automatically mean they would not be of interest to readers, but the perspective reflected in the editorial would largely be friendly to the advertisers' interest. Further, there are sections that would have limited reader interest, such as a focus on printing (in order that photocopy and other machines can be advertised around it).

Executives at the Special Projects Division are aware that the copy they produce does not have the same credibility as the stories in other sections of the newspapers. However, they assume that readers are aware that these sections are advertorial, and refer to the labelling of the sections – 'Special Feature', etc. – as the signal that alerts the reader. Our focus group research, however, though limited, does not show that readers are particularly perceptive about how such copy is generated (see Chapter 6). Moreover, the research shows that they are reading *The Star*, with its various sections and inserts, and will attribute to Special Projects sections the same credibility that they attribute to other sections of the paper.

If readers are not able to make the distinction between surveys and journalistic editorial, there is a need for concern about the impact of the special sections on the rest of the newspaper. As Tulleken and Meyer described it, the subjects of the features or surveys are often determined by trends in society or by the news of the day, covered in various media – *The Star* included. This means the editorial sections and the advertorial sections of the paper could carry reports on the same issues, which are produced in isolation from each other, thus raising the possibility of conflicting perspectives. These are demonstrated by the examples that we found in the short space of the research, where the approach to covering certain social issues and news stories differed between the news section and the advertorial sections, thus setting up a conflict between them. Many readers may not be able to make sense of such contradictions, and react by losing faith in the newspaper.

There is no doubt that this 'third arm' can produce an enormous amount of revenue for the publication it operates in, and that it has become a standard strategy for many publications. It could also be argued that there is some value to these sections, particularly if they bring more content to readers that would serve or interest them, or if they provide a way for government to communicate more effectively with its constituents. However, the research on Special Projects shows that this practice at newspapers needs to be used with care, and that the potential issues and problems that may arise need to be examined.

CHAPTER 6

Focus groups

To gain some insights into the ways readers may respond to advertorial, we ran four focus-group discussions about the Special Projects sections of *The Star*. These focus-group discussions were carried out with four groups of students from two universities to determine their understanding and perception of strategies used by newspapers and magazines to generate more income. As credibility is one of the concerns of this research, the focus group first set out to determine whether the students were aware of these strategies, whether they could distinguish between advertorial and editorial, what they thought about such practices, and how they imagined these strategies might affect newspapers and magazines and their readers.

The discussion was carried out with four groups, two groups each composed of five students and the other two each of seven students. The students were randomly selected and the discussions carried out on different days. The first and second group of five each, ten in total, comprised students taking first- and second-year media studies courses at Wits University in Johannesburg. The students, three male and seven female, were all studying towards a Bachelor of Arts degree; their ages ranged between 19 and 22 years.

The third and fourth groups of students were selected from the journalism department of the Tshwane University of Technology (TUT) in Pretoria. Fourteen students were randomly selected, seven from the first-year journalism programme, and the other seven from the second-year class. Each group comprised three boys and four girls, with ages ranging between 19 and 23.

The focus-group study was carried out in a form of structured informal discussion, in which the reading habits of the group were first established. This was done to get an appraisal of what they were reading, how they read and whether they were acquainted with the subject of our discussion. Then the procedure of the discussions was explained to the groups, without letting them know what the objectives were.

They were each given a section of *The Star* newspaper to point out what they thought were paid content or advertisements. Next, they were asked what they thought of such features in relation to the paper's credibility and the quest to meet the bottom line and, finally, how they thought these might affect the readers and the newspaper.

It was established that the students did read newspapers and magazines, albeit irregularly and not in great detail because of lack of interest and time. Most of them acknowledged that they mostly skimmed through the newspapers they read, looking at the headlines of stories inside and on the front pages. They also read a variety of daily and weekly papers and magazines, *The Star* included. They read generally the mainstream newspapers, with no particular preference for a paper or sections of a paper.

The students were each given a copy of a section of the March 2005 issues of *The Star*. The first group, those taking first-year media studies courses at Wits University, were given a copy of the inside section of *The Star*, which carries lifestyle articles, sports, opinion, comments and analysis and editorials. The second group was given the *Business Report* section. Both these sections contain advertorials marked as Special Projects Advertisement Features. The same was done for the groups in Pretoria. The first-year journalism students were each given a copy of the Verve Section, the same copies that were given to their first-year counterparts at Wits University, and the second years also got the *Business Report* section.

They were each asked to identify what they thought was 'paid content' in the paper. Some of them did not understand the meaning of paid content and it had to be explained to them that paid content in this case was any editorial content in the paper that somebody paid for so that it would appear. Still, some of them, the first-years especially, had problems determining what editorial was paid for and what was not. Though they could easily point out display advertisements, they had difficulty pointing out editorial that they thought was paid for. As one said, she was 'not really sure what was paid for and what was not,' especially in *Business Report's* company news section. One student at TUT pointed out that most stories seemed to focus on particular companies, which might mean that the companies could be paying for it.

As to the object of our interest – the Special Projects pages – only one student in all the focus groups combined was able to point out the Special Projects pages as paid for. He was the only student in the combined group of 24 students who had, prior to the discussions, taken note of the Special Projects Division features appearing frequently in *The Star* and other papers of the Independent Group, and had recognised them as advertorial.

Some of the other students said they had seen or noticed the sections, but had never realised that was paid-for content, while others said they had never seen them or taken note of them, thus they were not able to identify them during the discussions, even though they had been reading *The Star* for a while. One of the students of the second-year group at Wits University was able to identify the section as paid-for content during the process of discussing what the section was.

Asked what he thought about the advertisement features, the student who had prior knowledge about the Special Projects pages said he thought it was an attempt by the people who paid for it – government and businesses – to 'try to speak to the masses out there, and try to make the general public aware of certain things,' and also to inform the public 'how to use their services' – referring to business.

When it was explained to the other students what the Special Projects Division features were all about, some of them found the strategy strange. They acknowledged that it might be a good and effective way of reaching out and informing the public, giving them information from the perspective of the advertisers, and they found nothing wrong with that as long as the information was reliable and important to those who needed it.

One of them said: 'I think it is like a self-help page'. But another raised the question of whether the section served the purpose. Is it effective? Do people actually read it or get it as it is intended? This student added, 'because as a journalism student, I have never noticed it so my question is: do people actually read it?' Another felt that the fact that the advertisers had been putting their advertisements in regularly meant that they were reaching their target, that people were reading, but he would question the objectivity of the features as they were 'inclined to put the advertisers in a positive light'.

One second-year TUT student commented that the fact that the substance of these articles might contradict what appeared in the regular news sections might put the paper in a bad light as it could lose the 'focus of its audience'. Another said that what the features said to him was 'if you have enough money, you have the power to manipulate information, which is exactly what the advertisers are doing'. The question for him was: 'Why do the newspapers allow this ambiguity?'

Some thought it was thinly disguised advertising and should be clearly marked as such. One student remarked:

> Sometimes you pick up a newspaper or magazine and start reading, then all of a sudden, it looks uncannily like advertising because they are talking about just one person or product and then you look at the top of the page and it's written in fine print 'advertorial' and you feel like you [are] being duped because the newspapers/advertisers have tricked you into reading what normally you would not read.

Another said that the fact that they went through the pages and did not see that it was marked as advertorial meant that it was difficult for the public to know and as such they felt as though they had been fooled.

The discussion was then directed towards the question of credibility and objectivity, and they were asked if they found any problem with these kinds of strategy and if they might affect the newspapers and the readers.

The students expressed ethical concerns over the credibility and objectivity of these articles as they viewed such advertorial as biased towards the advertiser. One said, 'You are forced to read what they want. As such, they are dictating to the audience.' Another concurred, adding that the articles were not open to debate as other articles in the newspaper would be, getting both sides of a story, and thus the newspapers might be seen as being biased and might lose their credibility.

A student in the first group contended that she was not very concerned because some people might find the information provided useful, and also because newspapers are not entirely bound to be objective. 'I am not entirely sure if it makes the papers lose credibility, and I am not sure newspapers are out there to be 100 per cent credible. I believe that's why we have different kinds of newspapers,' she added. One concluded that, whatever the case, it was important that readers were informed and all information should be put out there, and left to the readers to determine which was which and make an informed decision.

To most of the students though, as a business model, special sections make sense as newspapers need to make money to keep afloat. But what is important to them and what they consistently pointed out is that the features, taken as a whole, would not be perceived as bad if the newspapers made sure that it they were clearly marked as such. One of them observed, 'People might not know that it is an ad and might just read the story without thinking too deeply about it … if we didn't notice it, what are the chances of ordinary people noticing it is an ad?'

Another argued that there was nothing fundamentally wrong with the Special Features sections, but people should be able to distinguish when it is advertorial. Otherwise, it might affect the credibility of the paper, because, as a reader, you cannot tell that the story is coming from somebody who has paid for it to be there.

CHAPTER 7

Interviews with magazine managers

Adspend took a giant leap in 2005, with total spending on advertising in the media more than double the total for 2001. In that year, total media adspend stood at R8 billion; today it stands at R17 billion. However, this has not necessarily translated into good news for consumer magazines, which have seen a steady decline of their share of adspend over the last five years. In 2001, consumer magazines commanded 14.2% of total adspend. It slid to 11.7% in 2002, to 11.5% in 2003 and stood at 9.2% in 2005 (Koenderman 2005: 9). One could argue that there is still more advertising revenue available for magazines because, although the share of advertising has declined, there is a big pie to be shared out. However, the number of magazines has almost doubled in the last decade, which means that competition for advertising has increased.

According to Rajay Ambekar, fund manager at African Harvest (see Mochiko 2006), the magazine market is overtraded. With more magazine titles on the stands, there is increased niching and segmentation of the market, which has led to a decrease of the share that individual magazines used to get. The increase in the total readership of all magazines has been small (SAARF 2006), which has meant more competition for readers, too. Sales and circulation figures of certain publications have been stagnant, if not declining, while others have grown.

The research set out to examine how publishers of magazines negotiate these conditions, particularly in relation to declining adspend. Through interviews of decision-makers at leading magazine groups in South Africa, we aimed to understand how they see the relationship between advertisers and magazine publishers, what strategies they have developed to attract advertising, and how these may influence the editorial decision-making process and the content of magazines. We also asked whether the magazine publishing groups have set guidelines or codes of conduct for advertising, advertorial and other kinds of linked content.

We interviewed Mike Tissong, General Manager of Johnnic Communications Media Magazine Division, Debbie McIntyre, Advertising Manager of Caxton Magazines, Jane Raphaely, the doyenne of South African magazine publishing, CEO of Associate Magazines and publisher of the South African *Cosmopolitan*, and Andrew Sneddon, Elsa Carpenter-Frank and Andrew Gillet of Touchline Publishing, a division of Media24 Magazines. Johncom, Caxton and Media24 are the biggest magazine publishers in South Africa (FIPP/Zenith 2004).

Specifically, we asked them how they perceived their relationship with advertisers, what kind of influence advertisers had over their publications, and what the standard practices were in the magazines in relation to advertorial, editorial and linked content. We also asked them what kinds of demand advertisers made and what policy guidelines they had in place to safeguard editorial integrity, including whether paid-for content was signalled to the reader.

All the interviewees agreed that advertising was absolutely essential to magazine publishing. As Jane Raphaely put it, 'I don't know of any successful magazine that has ever existed commercially without advertising'. Debbie McIntyre of Caxton Magazines agreed with this, saying this was the reason why advertisers have an influence in the market:

> They [advertisers] play a very important role, because without them, it would be very difficult for any magazine to survive. It is understandable then that they do put on a lot of pressure and carry a lot of weight because they put in a lot of money, and of course in such cases, you would want to have a say in how things go.

Elsa Carpenter-Frank, publisher of *Shape* magazine, said:

> [w]e rely on them heavily. Without them, we would not be able to have a business, but also I think the more niched your publication or the better your readership relationship to the magazine, the more valuable it is to the advertiser. But it works both ways as our readers also like to see the advertisement in the magazine because it's more like it is recommended by *Shape*.

Realising that they hold the purse strings and are key to the survival of these magazines, advertisers sometimes don't hesitate to use this as leverage to get what they want. Andrew Sneddon, publisher of *Men's Health* magazine, acknowledged this: 'They do sometimes push the envelope to see how far they can go with their demands'.

Even when there are no demands, magazine owners and publishers have also realised the situation they find themselves in. To stay afloat, they must convince the advertisers that their magazine is the best conduit to reach the targeted audience, and they don't hesitate to come up with various strategies to convince the advertisers to stay with them. However, the interviewees all claimed the relationship was nothing but business and professional. One thing they all had in common was that they supplied the advertisers with a target market for their products. Mike Tissong of Johncom's magazine division put it this way:

> We service them with niche products, we service them with specific communities of clients that would be most suited for their needs (we don't just come to them with a blanket number of clients that they cannot define) and we give them a defined client base that they can advertise to.

This relationship was sometimes cultivated over a number of years, and a kind of trust and understanding would develop between them, said Debbie McIntyre. Another important factor that characterises this relationship is the constant contact that they keep with the advertisers, informing them of new products, ideas and strategies. Since magazine production involves long-term planning, advertisers in most cases know months in advance what the contents of the magazines are going to be, so that they can decide whether they want to be associated with the issue, theme of the month, season or special sections.

According to Tissong, 'What we do is we establish themes twelve months ahead, saying that, for example, February we will be focusing on Valentine's Day and issues around relationships. Editorial is going to write on that and our advertising rep will go and sell on that'.

Another strategy involves the niching of the magazine titles to deliver a specific target audience, with a particular interest, to the advertisers. Debbie McIntyre said that, of the 11 magazines in the Caxton stable, 10 titles were consumer focused, particularly on women of a certain Living Standard Measure – that is, affluent women – and one was niched in the agricultural sector. Johncom Magazines are also consumer focused, their titles niched to serve an exclusive market. Tissong said that the reason for this was that, by niching publications, competition was reduced:

> So when you go to an advertiser with a proposition, it is unique enough to get a slice of the pie. It wouldn't be of value if you come up with a magazine where there are ten others operating in that field – then you got a problem on your hands. The key is to niche your titles.

Jane Raphaely saw this relationship in another light. For her, magazines served as a conduit for advertisers to reach an audience and, for that audience, the magazine was a shop window, where they could make choices, though she added that magazines did provide information and education around socio-economic and health issues.

> Remember that we are talking about a market and these are consumer magazines and that the role that they play in this market is to help people make informed choices … and enable them do their shopping, by providing them with information, where they can find all sorts of gifts, and other things that normally they would not have enough time to go look for. That is what magazines do for you.

She added that magazines employ people whose job it is to find what is new before the audience can find it:

> Thus, the journalist's job is to find out what the readers' problems would be next month, problems they haven't even thought of, and go out and try to find solutions to these problems and put it all in one package, so that the woman, when she gets her little half an hour to herself, she can go here and she can know that every month at least ten of her problems can be resolved by the magazines.

Thus, she said, the advertisers were invited to be part of this decision-making process of displaying their wares, using the magazines as a shop window.

> We actually invite them; because we actually need them to tell us before they do it what are they going to do next. So we sit with the people from Woolworths; we work three months in advance, at least, with Discovery, Standard Bank, etc., and say: 'What are you doing next? What is your strategy?' We are in continual communication with them, because we are in the same business. They are trying to improve their products to be more

competitive, to be more successful in the marketplace – we are their shop window.

This, she said, was what is called 'edited choice'.

On the question of editorial integrity and advertising, some publishers maintained that the two functions were kept separate, though they also acknowledged that commercial decisions did sometimes threaten the editorial integrity of the magazines.

For Johncom Magazines, the two functions were completely different and separated; the editorial people wrote what they felt would bring more readers, and that number of readers was used to leverage advertising into the magazines, said Mike Tissong. All interviewees accepted the fact that editors have the final say as far as editorial is concerned, mainly because of the need to be credible to the readers. The credibility of the magazine, said Debbie McIntyre, was something that the advertisers themselves also understood and knew they could not tamper with. As far credibility was concerned, Jane Raphaely said that they counted on the professionalism of the journalists, and relied on the fact the audience would not be fooled.

However, there appears to be no set of policy guidelines in the South African media industry to regulate the relationship between advertising and editorial and to stipulate what is and isn't acceptable. There are no clear policy guidelines such as those of the American Society of Magazine Editors (ASME), which deal with everything including design, what goes on the covers, sponsorships, editorial titles and staffing, and editorial and advertisement reviews. (See ASME Guidelines for Editors and Publishers 2006.) What does exist, particularly with regard to advertorials, is a sort of working understanding between most of the magazines and advertisers, such as having no logos on the advertorial page, and, if advertorial appears in several different titles, maintaining the same fonts and specifications. Editorially, journalists must adhere to the editorial guidelines of the magazines. Advertorial pages are often done with the help and participation of the staff of the magazines to help them conform to style.

Each publication, depending on the set-up of the organisation, is generally guided by what can be termed as acceptable unwritten practices. Mike Tissong observed the following:

> The only guides that we have are the themes. Thus even the advertisers are guided by the content that the readers must identify with. If the readers don't identify with the content that appeals [to] them, they are not going to buy that magazine, and if they don't buy that magazine, the advertisers are not going to get exposure, which both advertisers and editorials are fully aware of.

But this does not stop the advertisers from making demands or the publishers from making offers. Conflict does sometimes arise between an editorial stance and the demands of the advertisers, and, depending on the publication, it is dealt with in various ways. The reality of this conflict between editorial independence and advertisement consideration was brought to the fore in 2005 when, according to many news reports, Ann Donald, erstwhile editor of *Fair Lady* magazine, was forced to resign because she insisted on publishing a piece that might offend a major advertiser (Marshall 2005).

Debbie McIntyre explained as follows:

> Yes, they do have certain demands. What we try to do is to find common ground, around which we can work out a solution that serves both ways … sometimes we try to make the advertisers see that what is written is not necessarily about them in particular. We try to approach subjects in such a way that it does not seem like we are making a particular case or singling out somebody. We try to give it a general perspective. We try to give a fair overview and balance it.

Sometimes, though, the magazines just tried to ignore certain contentious subjects. Elsa Carpenter-Frank said, 'one tries not to go there', but she acknowledged that there were often conflicts between the commercial side and the editorial side, as editorial always want to write things and expose what they think should be exposed, while the advertisers try 'to push it' sometimes – try to make the magazines their mouthpieces.

There is also pressure from the in-house advertising team that comes up with new ideas for the advertisers, and they push the editor for certain kinds of article and feature. Andrew Gillet, publisher of *SA Sports Illustrated*, said the advertising department came up with ideas all the time 'because it is their job':

> If the advertisers or [the advertising department] see a possible angle on a story, they bring it to the editor and it is his call … If we can help out the advertiser and push their sponsorship further, fine, but every time the decision has to be: Is it right for the readers? Is it going to help us sell the magazine?

Although most of the interviewees said the editor had the final say over content, it became clear from the interviews that this is not always the case when it involved a major sponsor or advertiser. That decision was in the hands of the publisher, whose role, said Elsa Carpenter-Frank, was 'ensuring profitability of the magazines'.

Andrew Sneddon concurred:

> If there's anything that is a little contentious, he'll come around and have a chat with me about it. I'll have the final say, but he runs the magazine in terms of editorial. But if it's anything that might affect the magazine financially, he'll come and talk to me about it. He could be overruled, but at the end of the day, he decides what is good for the reader.

CHAPTER 8

Regulation

> Vigilant self-regulation is the hallmark of a free and independent Press
> (*Press Code of Professional Practice*)

Unlike the broadcast media in South Africa, the print sector is largely unregulated, based on the understanding that it regulates itself. Newspapers, for instance, are specifically excluded from the Films and Publications Act (No. 65 of 1996), including subsequent amendments of the act. This act monitors the content, publication and conditions of sale of all sex-related published material. It also controls the dissemination of images propagating war, violence or hatred. Chapter 6, Section 22(3), of the act states that 'A newspaper published, and a poster of a newspaper issued as an advertisement of any newspaper, by a publisher who is a member of the Newspaper Press Union of South Africa, shall not be subject to the provisions of this Act'.

The Newspaper Press Union (NPU) has since been dissolved and replaced by the umbrella body known as the Print Media Association (PMA) of South Africa. The Newspaper Association of South Africa, the closest structure to what used to be known as the NPU, now falls under the PMA. Though excluded specifically from the Films and Publications Act, newspapers are regulated by the press code. This code is governed by the 'founding bodies' of the industry, including the PMA, and regulates the practice of every newspaper and magazine in the country.

The press code is policed by the Press Ombudsman, currently former South African Press Association editor Ed Linnington. Complaints that cannot be resolved by individual titles are referred to the ombudsman for mediation and then for adjudication. In agreeing to take a grievance to the ombudsman, the complainant agrees that legal action is not being contemplated and waives any rights to claim civil relief. A range of punitive measures can be used by the ombudsman should a newspaper or magazine be found to be acting contrary to the code. These include a reprimand, the publication of a correction or apology or 'any supplementary or ancillary orders or directions that he or it may consider necessary for carrying into effect orders or directives made in terms of this clause and, more particularly, giv[ing] directions as to the publication of his/her or its findings' (POSA n.d. Constitution: 8).

However, the code makes no direct comment on the treatment of advertising in newspapers and magazines, possibly because it is designed to regulate editorial matters on the assumption that these operate in a separate arena from advertising. Thus, it leaves the membrane between the two entirely porous and, according to the press code at least, at the discretion of individual editors or companies. The code does, however, demand truthful, accurate and fair reportage in which 'only what may reasonably be true … may be presented as facts'. It adds, furthermore, that 'where a report is not based on facts or is founded on opinions, allegation, rumour or supposition, it shall be presented in such manner as to indicate this clearly'. In addition, the code demands the clear distinction between fact and opinion and requires that no distortion, misrepresentation or suppression of fact takes place (POSA n.d. Press Code of Professional Practice: 18). However, an editorial code may not necessarily be the place to regulate commercial workplace practices that are the result of company policies.

There are other elements to the regulatory environment of the South African print media, and these are worth setting out. There are a large number of laws and regulations relating to the media, including the 1996 Constitution, the Promotion of Access to Information Act (No. 2 of 2000), the Lotteries Act (No. 57 of 1997), the Competition Act (No. 89 of 1998) and the Independent Communications Authority of South Africa Act (No. 13 of 2000). None of these binds the print media to guidelines or limits on the use, display or labelling of paid-for content.

The PMA is also a member of ASASA, and thereby commits itself to ASASA's code. This code, according to ASASA, is based upon the International Code of Advertising Practice and is internationally accepted as the basis for domestic systems of regulation (www.asasa.org.za). According to ASASA, 'Advertising is a service to the public and, as such, should be informative, factual, honest, decent and its content should not violate any of the laws of the country'.

There are several sections of the ASASA code that deal with the labelling or identification of paid-for content or advertising. Section II, clause 4.2.1, deals with misleading claims, and states that 'advertisements should not contain any statement or visual presentation which, directly or by implication, omission, ambiguity, inaccuracy, exaggerated claim or otherwise, is likely to mislead the consumer'. The treatment of advertising material in a way that makes it closely resemble editorial content may, according to this clause, be construed as misleading and therefore contrary to the ASASA code. The code's attitude to the aping of editorial by paid-for content is once again highlighted under Section II in clause 12. This short passage is entitled 'Identification of Advertisements' and states the following:

- 12.1 Advertisements should be clearly distinguishable as such whatever their form and whatever the medium used. When an advertisement appears in a medium which contains news, editorial or programme matter it should be so designed, produced and presented that it will readily be recognised as an advertisement.
- 12.2 In print media, wherever there is any possibility of confusion, the material in question should be headed conspicuously with the words ADVERTISEMENT or ADVERTISEMENT SUPPLEMENT, and should be boxed in or otherwise distinguished from surrounding or accompanying editorial matter. (ASASA n.d.: Section II: 7)

In this way, the code unambiguously sets out the so-called Chinese Wall between advertising and editorial in the print media: advertising should simply be 'clearly distinguishable'. But perhaps the clearest declaration of all on this subject within the ASASA code can be found in a special section, Section V, entitled: 'Identification of editorial style print advertisements'. Here the code specifically sets out the rules and requirements to be followed when paid-for space is presented in an editorial style. This section reads as follows:

1. There is an obligation on all concerned with the preparation and/or publication of a print advertisement to ensure that anyone who looks at the advertisement is able to see, without reading it closely, that it is an advertisement and not editorial matter.
2. In the case of a single advertisement occupying a whole page or part of a page, the following guidelines are laid down:
    2.1 The word ADVERTISEMENT should stand alone at the head of the advertisement in such size and weight of type to be easily seen.
    2.2 If the advertisement occupies less than half a page, it should be boxed in completely or if half-page or more, separated from any adjacent matter by a distinct border.
    2.3 Particular care should be taken wherever the size and style of type in the advertisement is the same as, or closely resembles that of editorial matter.
3. Where paid-for space is in the style of editorial, whether paid for by the same or different advertisers, particular care is needed to ensure that no part can be mistaken for editorial matter.
4. As a general rule, where an advertisement or series of advertisements paid for by the same organisation or by organisations under the same control extends over more than one page, the word ADVERTISEMENT should be printed at the head of each page in such a way that a reader cannot fail to see it. Similarly, where a supplement is paid for wholly by an advertiser or advertisers, it should normally be headed in bold letters with the words ADVERTISING SUPPLEMENT, and carry the word(s) ADVERTISEMENT or ADVERTISING SUPPLEMENT at the head of each page.
5. No guidance can cover every case. It may not be enough merely to follow to the letter what is said above. It may also be necessary to look again at each advertisement to see whether it is clearly distinguishable from the editorial content of the publication in which it appears and if not to take steps to ensure that it is. (ASASA n.d.: Section V)

This section of the advertising code (Section V), supported by clauses 12 and 4.2.1 in Section II, clearly defines the regulatory framework within which print organisations are obliged to present advertising and editorial material. Sanctions for contravening the code vary from the immediate withdrawal of the advertisement to the compulsory pre-vetting of all proposed advertisements for a six-month period. Surprisingly, however, in the seven years since records were computerised at ASASA, only one ruling has been made on a complaint laid against a newspaper with regard to the editorial-style manner in which advertising material was presented.[9] This was a matter between *The People's Post* (Fish Hoek Printing and Publishing CC) and the Noordhoek Environmental Action Group (NEAG) that took place in early 2002 (ASA Database, Complaint 4100, 8 January 2002).

---

9 Discussion with Gail Schimmel, Head of Legal & Regulatory Affairs, ASASA, June 2006.

In its complaint, NEAG said an article had been published by *The People's Post*, 'which is clearly a promotional feature/advertisement ... without any reference to that being the case'. NEAG cited all the sections listed above: Section II, clause 4.2.1 (Misleading claims), Section II, clause 12 (Identification of advertisements) and Section V (Identification of editorial style print advertisements). The ASASA directorate upheld the complaint, ruling that 'as the respondent's advertising does not comply with the sections of the Code it is deemed to be in contravention' (ASASA Database, Complaint 4100, 8 January 2002). The offending advertising was ordered withdrawn with immediate effect.

The question must then be posed as to why more contraventions have not been brought to ASASA's attention in this regard. After all, it is apparent that, in terms of the relevant sections of the ASASA code, a *prima facie* case exists against many South African print media titles regarding the manner in which paid-for content is displayed and signalled. Yet, other than *The People's Post*, not a single contravention has been reported in more than seven years. The key here is the complaint, as ASASA will not act unless a formal complaint has been lodged – and nobody has complained. This may be due to a low level of awareness around the issue both within the industry and in society. This highlights the need for editors, media managers, advertising executives and the public at large to be sensitised to a practice that is demonstrably discouraged internationally (the ASASA code is based on international codes) as being ethically unsound. Indeed, it appears that many editors or members of senior editorial management in South Africa are not aware of these elements of the ASASA code, do not take note of it at all in day-to-day decision making around commissioning and content or do not understand that they are bound by it.

Part of the problem, however, may also be that advertising takes many different forms, only one of which is aping the editorial style of respected print media titles. These forms of paid-for content are not specifically covered by the ASASA code. One form of advertising is, for example, the unsignalled use of a client's image on the cover of a magazine. Other situations not covered by the code include editorial teams undertaking the writing of the advertorial copy, sometimes under their own by-lines, advertising space being marketed to coincide with linked content, free content being included on the basis of a political or other agenda, and decisions being taken with regard to what is put in or left out of editorial to match advertisers' expectations. While the code's principle of making non-editorial material 'clearly distinguishable' holds true, the complexity and diversity of advertising vehicles and processes exacerbates levels of non-compliance that are already high. If, for instance, articles are generated and published on the basis that they provide the context for advertising, this makes it difficult to apply the code to the offending material.

The end result is a code, and indeed a regulatory framework, that is simply not coping with the new trends and new demands of the South African print media. The current ASASA code unambiguously states the undesirability of advertising feigning editorial, spells out the requirements and penalties and has even ruled against the one newspaper about which it has received a complaint. Yet, because of ASASA's dependence on complaints, poor awareness within and beyond the industry and rapid changes and increasing complexity in advertising processes, the code has little regulatory force. With the ASASA code unable to regulate advertorial in the industry, and with no other codes, laws or regulations that appear to impact on the practice, the South African print media sector has been left vulnerable to a potentially damaging global development.

Having said this, there does appear to be some evidence that journalists and media executives involved in advertorial sense that a change is needed. *The Star* newspaper, one of the case studies in this monograph, has codes that regulate advertising sections and surveys (Independent Newspapers 2006), and the Independent Group is considering drawing up a charter to regulate special projects sections across the group.[10] It is the authors' belief that most South African journalists and editors want to behave ethically, and have a strong adherence to the idea that media have a responsibility to promote the interests of the public. Many of these journalists feel that there has been a deterioration of editorial integrity in recent years as new products, new technology and new demands have forced decision makers increasingly into ethical grey areas. We would argue that it is time for a debate around such issues, with a particular focus on how to manage potentially damaging or unethical situations. Among the topics for consideration would be whether publications should produce their own codes of practice around advertorial, and whether the industry should look at producing an industry-wide set of guidelines to guide decision making in the grey area of paid-for content.

---

10 Personal communication with Andrew Cuthbertson, Independent Media.

CHAPTER 9

Conclusion

Competition for advertising revenue and changes in marketing approaches and media products in the last decade have led to a rapidly changing business environment for print media. In this context, many publications have explored and instituted new ways of attracting advertising revenue. Foremost among these approaches is a focus on developing and devising new forms of paid-for content, including the use of sections and supplements that are targeted to attract advertising and the packaging together of editorial content and advertising material for sale to advertisers.

In this research we sought to examine these commercial developments, and to consider the possible implications for media credibility and for the media's normative role in society. We tried to get a sense of the range of strategies being employed by publications, of the problems and practices that may arise from such strategies, and of the potential consequences for the content, for the readers and for journalistic practice. We also asked to what extent the commercial media regulate and manage paid-for content, and whether the industry needs to consider creating new codes or adapting existing codes to set general guidelines for ethical behaviour in this regard.

A particular focus of the research was signalling – the practice of clearly marking advertising copy as 'Advertisement'. We wanted to explore the perception that many publications appear to be failing to signal adequately to readers when the content they are reading has been paid for by advertisers and when it has not. As part of this investigation, we asked the question whether certain kinds of content carried in publications purely to attract advertising cannot easily be identified as such, and whether more rigorous adherence to signalling, which is required by ASASA, would address some of the ethical concerns about linked content. Finally, we wanted to get a sense of whether readers were able to distinguish between content that is generated by journalistic editorial values and content that is produced in order to attract advertising revenue, and what they may think of such content.

As pointed out in the methodology section, the project was necessarily limited in scope. The case studies attempted to map the prevalence and packaging of linked content in three publications – all very different from each other – looking at the impact of strategies to attract advertising along the chain of production. We were aware that the results could not be generalised to all publications, but that the research could reveal the issues and situations faced by publications, the choices they make to deal with them, and the effects of those choices on content.

The research across all the cases found that all the publications used some form of advertorial or linked content, but each publication had a different set of guidelines and practices for such content. The constellation of strategies that they used also differed from one another, which indicated that all publications do not do the same things, but adapt their products to suit their particular circumstances.

Both *Finance Week* and the Independent Group newspapers separated the general editorial section from the advertising department; however, they had separate advertising salespeople and writers for the sections carrying paid-for or linked content. What the first two examples indicate is that the so-called Chinese Wall between editorial and paid-for content still stands, but that a third arm of content generation has been developed, where advertising and editorial are conceived of together and there is no separation between people selling advertising and those producing editorial.

Problems with the development of a third arm of content production, however, became clear from a content analysis of *The Star*. In the time period of the research, two examples were found of evident contradictions between stories produced by the newsroom and stories produced by the Special Projects Division. This is a potential problem for credibility, and it is an indication of the way in which paid-for content can have a negative impact on journalistic content even though it is produced separately. There was no obvious impact of paid-for content on editorial content in the other publications, but the potential is clearly there for such conflicts to develop or even for a diluting effect on editorial if special sections are not of the standard of the rest of the publication.

If one accepts that the traditional way of doing business in newspapers was to separate editorial and advertising, then of interest here is the development of this new and additional practice, which continues to keep the mainstream editorial and advertising apart, but has a third arm for special sections. This new division in a media business develops and blurs advertising, public relations and journalism in an effort to attract more advertising revenue, and to produce readable content that looks and feels like editorial. The case studies demonstrated that the third arm has become an important strategy to attract advertising revenue, and that publications will increasingly be developing such sections as part of their normal commercial operations. However, it also demonstrates that there are dangers in this practice that have not yet been fully engaged with, and that the media industry needs to examine ways in which these potential problems can be managed.

Also of interest in the research is the way in which practice is influenced by perceptions of the readership. *Finance Week* very explicitly states that the appearance of advertising and editorial being linked needs to be avoided as they believe their readers would notice and would not like it. They signal advertorial content when it appears. They are less concerned, though, about sections where advertising and editorial are linked by theme; that is, where the section has been produced to attract advertising rather than readers. For quality publications like this, credibility is protected by ethical practice in relation to the more usual forms of paid-for content; the area of concern would be around themed sections and ways to deal with those. Specifically, there needs to be a focus on whether the themed sections do add value to the publication and the readers, or whether they are simply there for advertising.

Staff at the Independent Group's Special Projects Division also believed that readers could tell the difference between editorial in the sections they produced and editorial produced by the newsroom. This, they felt, protected them from accusations of misleading the reader. However, in the focus groups of media students, readers displayed a clear lack of understanding of what these advertorial sections were and a discomfort with the idea that copy they had been reading in good faith as journalistic was, in fact, paid for. Some indicated that they did not mind the practice of running such sections, as long as they were informative, but felt that paid-for content should be signalled to the reader. The inability of these readers to recognise paid-for content does raise the question of exactly how media-savvy general readers actually are, and whether producers of advertorial sections can generally assume that their readers know where the content comes from. If they do not, then advertorial producers cannot rely on reader comprehension as a defence.

To get a broader idea of the way in which publications see their relationship with advertisers and how they try to manage that relationship, we interviewed media executives at five of the largest magazine companies in the country, owners of more than 70 per cent of local magazines. They were asked about the conditions under which they operate, the strategies they use to attract advertising across all their titles, and whether there were codes for regulating advertising decisions for their publications.

All the executives agreed that advertising was absolutely crucial to the survival of their publications, and that some advertisers and, sometimes, the publication's own in-house advertising salespeople would put pressure on the editorial sections to meet certain demands. All executives also agreed that magazines operated very much in niches, specifically targeting audiences that advertisers want ('a defined client base').[11] Some argued that advertising provided readers with information, making their publications a 'shop window'.[12]

Unlike newspapers, where there is still a strict division between advertising and editorial and the editor has the final say over editorial content, and where sections of advertorial/paid-for content are run separately, magazines do not generally apply such a strict separation. Groups such as Johnnic Communications still operate with a strict division, but other magazines keep advertisers in mind as they produce stories for publication. One interviewee admitted that her magazines sometimes stayed away from contentious subjects because of possible fallout from advertising, and that, if advertisers objected to any editorial content, they would meet with them and try to persuade them of the publication's point of view. This indicates that advertisers can and do influence copy, and that editors and journalists operate with this in mind. In many of the companies, the publisher, rather than the editor, has the last word if there are problems with editorial that could lose revenue for the magazine. The separation between editorial and advertising functions at many magazines, then, appears to be something of a light picket fence. No written codes or guidelines are

---

11 Interview with Mike Tissong. See Chapter 7.
12 Interview with Jane Raphaely. See Chapter 7.

used by any magazine company to regulate the relationship between advertising and editorial.

In conclusion, the most significant issue raised by the research generally is the impact of paid-for content on the overall editorial focus or identity of a publication. Content driven by advertising imperatives can deviate from or dilute the primary orientation of the newspaper or magazine, which has traditionally been directed at serving readers and building a relationship with them. This can decrease the value of a publication in the eyes of readers, who can lose interest in it if they have to wade through content that does not interest them, or lose faith in it if they begin to doubt its credibility. The loss of readers is a serious potential consequence that is important not just to publishers and journalists but to the advertisers in the publication.

It follows, then, that a great deal more attention needs to be given to the role of the reader in advertising-editorial relationships. The focus groups indicated that the media students understood little about the internal operations of publications and the ways in which they influence content, that they were unable to recognise paid-for content, and that they felt uneasy about its appearance in the publication. However, some indicated a preparedness to tolerate paid-for content that did not particularly interest them if it contributed to the overall commercial well-being of the publication, in much the same way that they would accept display advertisements. Because the focus groups are not representative of the broader reading population, more research needs to be done to investigate what readers actually know about the workings of publications, what they expect from them, and how they read paid-for content. Further, it would be useful to investigate what kinds of paid-for content readers will accept and at what point paid-for content begins to alienate them.

The findings of this pilot project indicate the need for a sustained and detailed discussion about the treatment of paid-for content in print media, in order to understand better the implications of the variety of practices associated with this strategy. Certain media groups are already recognising the need for such self-examination, including the Independent Group (featured in this research), which is in the process of drawing up a charter to regulate its Special Projects section. We would like to see a wider discussion, in which the industry considers whether an industry-wide code or set of guidelines is necessary, or in which its members consider drawing up codes for their own companies.

REFERENCES

ASASA (Advertising Standards Authority of South Africa) (n.d.) *Code of advertising practice.* Accessed 6 June 2006 at www.asasa.org.za/Default.aspx?mnu_id=70

ASME (American Society of Magazine Editors) (2006) *Guidelines for editors and publishers.* Accessed 5 July 2006 at www.magazine.org/Editorial/Guidelines

Bagdikian B (2000) *The media monopoly.* 6th edition. Boston, Massachusetts: Beacon Press

Becker J (ed) (1989) *Telefonieren.* Marburg: Jonas

Bogart L (1989) *Press and public: Who reads what, when, where and why in American newspapers.* 2nd edition. Hillsdale, New Jersey: Erlbaum

Choo S (2004) Increasing circulation follows investments in newsroom. *Newspaper Research Journal* 25(4): 1–9

Cowling L (2004) The rising sense of unease, *Rhodes Journalism Review* 24: 34–35

Crotty A (2006) *Media groups look after own interests.* Accessed July 27 2006 at www.journalism.co.za/modules.php?op=modload&name=News&file=article&sid=3555

Curran J & Seaton J (1991) *Power without responsibility: The press and broadcasting in Britain.* 4th edition. London: Routledge

De Beer AS & Prince E (2005) (eds) Focus on journalism, education and training, *Ecquid Novi* 26(2): 139–141

Dlamini N (2003) *News for sale in the business press: A look at Finance Week.* Accessed 3 May 2006 at www.journalism.co.za/modules.php?op=modload&name=News&file=article&sid=978

Duncan J (2003) Another journalism is possible: Critical challenges for the media in South Africa. Harold Wolpe Lecture Series, 30 October 2003. Accessed 14 July 2006 at www.ukzn.ac.za/ccs/default.asp?11,22,5,341

Edmonds R (2004) News staffing, news budgets and news capacity, *Newspaper Research Journal*, Winter 2004

Ensor L (2001) Ad agency calls for watchdog. *Business Day*, 11 July 2001. Accessed 28 July 2006 at www.businessday.co.za/Articles/TarkArticle.aspx?ID=467682

Finweek (2006) Readership profile. Accessed 28 July 2006 at www.fin24.co.za/downloads/FINWEEK/DOCS/FINWEEK_RP2006.pdf

FIPP/Zenith (International Federation of the Periodical Press/Zenith Optimedia) (2004) *World magazine trends handbook 2003/2004.* London: FIPP

Gallagher C (2005) Slumlords invade Johannesburg. *The Star*, 5 February 2005: 1

Garnham N (1990) *Capitalism and communication: Global culture and the economics of Information.* London: Sage

Gladney GA (1990) Newspaper excellence: How editors of small and large papers judge quality. *Newspaper Research Journal* 11(2): 60–72

Golding P & Murdock G (2000) Culture, communications and political economy. In J Curran & M Gurevitch (eds) *Mass media and society*. London: Edward Arnold

Habermas J (1989) *The structural transformation of the public sphere*. Cambridge: Polity Press

Harber A (2002) Journalism in the age of the market. Harold Wolpe Lecture, 26 September 2002. Accessed 20 June 2006 at www.nu.ac.za/ccs/default.asp

Harber A (2004) State warns of bottom-line threat. *Business Day*, 17 August 2004. Accessed 5 June 2006 at www.businessday.co.za/Articles/TarkArticle.aspx?ID=1163895

Harber A (2006) Can motoring journos change gear? *The Harbinger*. Accessed 20 June 2006 at www.big.co.za/wordpress/2006/03/07/can-motoring-journos-change-gear

Herman ES & Chomsky N (1994) *Manufacturing consent: The political economy of the mass media*. London: Vintage

Independent Newspapers (2006) Code of conduct for *The Star* surveys and advertising features. Accessed 28 July 2006 at www.journalism.co.za/modules.php?op=modload&name=News&file=article&sid=1772

Independent Online (2006) Accessed 28 July 2006 at www.iol.co.za

Jacobs S (2004) Public sphere, power and democratic politics: Media and policy debates in post-apartheid South Africa. Unpublished doctoral thesis. Birkbeck College, University of London

Kim K-H (2005) Survey yields five factors of newspaper quality. *Newspaper Research Journal*, Winter 2005. Department of Journalism, University of Memphis. Accessed 20 July 2006 at www.findarticles.com/p/articles/mi_qa3677/is_200501/ai_n13634100

Koenderman T (2001) *Financial Mail*, 8 June 2001

Koenderman T (2005) South Africa: Media, facts, insights, ideas, results. In T. Koenderman, *Ad Review* 2005: 9

Lacy S & Fico F (1991) The link between newspaper content quality and circulation, *Newspaper Research Journal* 12(2): 46–57

Leonard T (2000) The wall: A long history, *Columbia Journalism Review* 38(5): 28

Lockyear H (2004) Multiculturalism in South African soap operas, *Communicatio* 30(1): 26–43

Louw E (2001) *The media and cultural production*. London: Sage

Louw J (2005) Journalism and the law. In A Hadland (ed) *Changing the fourth estate: Essays on South African journalism*. Cape Town: HSRC Press

Mansell R (1993) *The new telecommunications: A political economy of network evolution*. London: Sage

Marshall S (2005) *Fair Lady* editors don't just go quietly. *The Media Online*, 2 November 2005. Accessed 10 November 2005 at www.themedia.co.za/article.aspx?articleid=255564&area=/media_news

References

McManus JH (1994) *Market-driven journalism: Let the citizen beware?* London: Sage

McQuail D (1987) *Mass communication theory: An introduction*. 2nd edition. London: Sage

Meyer PE (2003) Quality journalism and the bottom line, *Proceedings of the ASNE convention* (American Society of Newspaper Editors) New Orleans, April 2003

Meyer PE (2004) *The vanishing newspaper: Saving journalism in the information age*. Columbia and London: University of Missouri Press

Mochiko T (2006) Adspend doubles to R1bn in five years, *Business Report*, 2 March 2006. Accessed 10 March 2006 at www.busrep.co.za/index.php?fArticleId=3137240

Morgan F (2004) The price of freedom: Professional capability, *Communicatio* 30(1): 15–25

Mosco V (1996) *The political economy of communication: Rethinking and renewal*. London: Sage

O'Neill O (2002) A question of trust, *Reith Lectures* 1–5. Accessed 9 February 2006 at www.bbc.co.uk/print/radio4/reith2002

Picard RG (1985) *The press and the decline of democracy*. Westport, Connecticut: Greenwood Press

POSA (Press Ombudsman of South Africa) (n.d.) Press Code of Professional Practice. Accessed 6 February 2006 at www.ombudsman.org.za/content/default.asp

SAARF (South African Advertising Research Foundation) (2006) *Magazine readership trends*. Accessed 28 July 2006 at www.saarf.co.za

SAHRC (South African Human Rights Commission) (2000) *Faultlines: Inquiry into racism in the media*. Johannesburg: SAHRC

Schudson M (1984) *Advertising, the uneasy persuasion: Its dubious impact on American society*. New York: Basic Books

Schudson M (1995) *The power of news*. Cambridge, Massachusetts: Harvard University Press

Siebert FS Peterson T & Schramm W (1956) *Four theories of the press*. Urbana, Illinois: University of Illinois Press

Smythe D (1981) *Dependency Road: Communications, capitalism, consciousness and Canada*. Norwood, New Jersey: Ablex

Special Projects reporter (2005) *The Star* (Verve section), 10 March, 2005: 15

South Africa Info (2006) *The press in South Africa*. Accessed 28 July 2006 at www.southafrica.info/ess_info/sa_glance/media/news.htm

Steenveld L (2004) Transforming the media: A cultural approach, *Critical Arts* 18(1): 92–115

Steinem G (1990) Sex, lies and advertising. *MS*, July/August 1990: 18–28

Stone GC Stone DB & Trotter E (1981) Newspaper quality's relation to circulation, *Newspaper Research Journal* 2(3): 16–24

Taylor A (2002) BDFM's Pottinger looks at new print philosophy. *Business Day*, 15 February 2002. Accessed 28 July 2006 at www.businessday.co.za/Articles/TarkArticle.aspx?ID=496367

Thorson E (2003a) News content quality, newsroom expenditures, circulation/penetration and revenue. Presentation at the American Society of Newspaper Editors (ASNE) convention, New Orleans, April 2003. Accessed 1 May 2003 at www.asne.org/index.cfm?ID=4467

Thorson E (2003b) Quality journalism and the bottom line. *Proceedings of the ASNE convention*, New Orleans, April 2003. Accessed 8 December 2006 at www.asne.org/index.cfm?ID=5629

TRC (Truth and Reconciliation Commission) (1998) *Truth and Reconciliation Commission Report 1998. Institutional Hearing: the Media*, Volume 4, Chapter 6. Cape Town: Truth and Reconciliation Commission

Ueckermann H (2005) The impact of income-generating strategies at newspapers: A study of *Geld*. Unpublished master's thesis: University of the Witwatersrand

Van Ginneken J (1998) *Understanding global news: A critical introduction*. London: Sage